How would Society Cope with Another Financial Crisis

How would Society Cope with Another Financial Crisis

Nicholas Clark

authorHOUSE®

AuthorHouse™ LLC
1663 Liberty Drive
Bloomington, IN 47403
www.authorhouse.com
Phone: 1-800-839-8640

© 2014 Nicholas Clark. All rights reserved.

No part of this book may be reproduced, stored in a retrieval system, or
transmitted by any means without the written permission of the author.

Published by AuthorHouse 7/28/2014

ISBN: 978-1-4969-3033-0 (sc)
ISBN: 978-1-4969-3032-3 (hc)
ISBN: 978-1-4969-3034-7 (e)

Library of Congress Control Number: 2014913455

Any people depicted in stock imagery provided by Thinkstock are models,
and such images are being used for illustrative purposes only.
Certain stock imagery © Thinkstock.

This book is printed on acid-free paper.

Because of the dynamic nature of the Internet, any web addresses or links contained in
this book may have changed since publication and may no longer be valid. The views
expressed in this work are solely those of the author and do not necessarily reflect the views
of the publisher, and the publisher hereby disclaims any responsibility for them.

Contents

Abstract xi

CHAPTER 1 INTRODUCTION 1

   1.1 Introduction 1

   1.2 Understanding the Financial Crisis 3

   1.3 Great Depression and Great Recession 4

   1.4 Gap 8

   1.5 Thesis and Theme Justification 10

   1.6 Methodology and Thesis Structure 11

   1.7 Conclusion 14

CHAPTER 2 PRE-CRISES ENVIRONMENT 16

   2.1 Introduction 16

   2.2 The Stimulating Resemblances 17

   Redundant Spending 22

   2.3 Outstanding Obliviousness 33

   2.4 Conclusion 34

CHAPTER 3 POST CRISES ENVIRONMENT: HAS THE PROBLEM BEEN EFFICIENTLY MANAGED? 35

3.1 Introduction 35

3.2 The impacts of the Crises 36

3.3 The overall Response to the Crises 46

3.3.1 Policies 47

3.3.2 Protectionism and Structural Differences 51

3.4 Lessons from Global Financial Crises 52

3.4.1 The Regulatory Bodies are Built on very Weak Theoretical Foundation 53

3.4.2 Widespread Perverse Incentives 53

3.4.3 Underwriting Matters 54

3.4.4 The Unregulated and Unsupervised Financial Institutions 56

3.5 Conclusion 57

CHAPTER 4 COPING WITH ANOTHER GLOBAL FINANCIAL CRISIS: IS THERE NEED FOR NEW BODIES 60

4.1 Introduction 60

4.2 Economic Perspective 61

4.4 Is There need for New Institutions? 77

4.4.1 Capabilities of the Current Regulatory Bodies 78

4.4.2 Can Rules be set without New Institutions? 79

4.5 Conclusion 80

CHAPTER 5 CONCLUSION 83

    5.1 Introduction 83

    5.2 Summary... 83

    5.3 Way Forward 87

    5.4 Conclusion 90

References... 91

For my wife Georgia and children, Mitchell, Lucy, and Elliot. Your patience, love and support have kept me going.

Also, to Gavin, Craig (Goose) and Craig Metz for your friendship, loyalty, education and guidance, which without, this paper would not have been achieved.

Abstract

The purpose of this thesis paper is to analyze the effects of the two major economic crises, the Great Depression and the Global Financial Crisis of 2008, with a focus on the social and ecological aspects.

The pre-crises environment shows that there are stimulating resemblances of the Great Depression and the Great Recession. The similarities of the Great Depression and the Great Recession tends to also indicate that their causes are also similar to each other. The two financial crises are characterized by a boom that results from making economic mistakes, and it is during the bust that the mistakes can be corrected. The two crises are a classic examples of the undesirable unintended consequences of government intervention, not only through expansionary monetary policy, but also through misguided attempts to bolster the prevailing market conditions.

The analysis of post crises environment shows that the two financial crises resulted to a significant increase in unemployment which affected workers disproportionately. Various response mechanisms were initiated in order to make countries to stand again on their feet, as well as help them develop shock absorbers in case of such an occurrence. Other responses to the crises includes use of protectionism and structural differences, and policy formulations. The failure of the current regulatory bodies is also quite evident as seen in through the study. The current regulatory bodies failed to operate the financial regulatory body and did not manage to coordinate a reliable supervision of the financial entities.

Inherently, to work their way out or avoid other crises in the future, there is need for government and regulators then of having more coordination in regulatory policies at a global level and also government getting out of regulatory systems in order to engage a free market. Further, having a free banking system is likely to stop the credit expansions that normally generates the boom and the bust cycle, which are accompanied by recessions, as noted by the Austrian theory.

Chapter 1
INTRODUCTION

1.1 Introduction

From time to time in history events of seismic significance occurs, and they mark a turning point between one epoch and another. However, the significance of most of these events is not clear when they are unfolding, but they become apparent only in retrospect. One of the agents behind these events is the global financial crisis. The global financial crises has in the last century been one of the main assaults of the global economic stability to have occurred. It basically describes the regulatory failure in the modern history. More importantly, it is more than a crisis in the debt markets, credit markets, property markets, equity markets and derivation markets. It is a financial crisis that has results to general economic crisis, such as the unemployment crisis, and in many countries, it can brought along social crisis as well as ecological crisis. The world is currently struggling to recover from the aftermath of the worst economic crisis ever since the Great Depression.

The World of the 21st century has witnessed various financial and economic crises. The downfall of the macroeconomic indicators in the globalized market has led to shrinking in most of the nations' productiveness, accompanied by the falling of consumption, purchasing power as well as the inflation and high number of bankruptcies, along with skyrocketing rate of unemployment.'

The occurrence of the Global Financial Crisis of 2007 -2008 rekindled the memories of a similar financial crisis, the Great Depression, in 1930s. The two financial crises have had profound effects, much more than anticipated by many. The national borders were breached and the ramifications were felt very far from the epicenter (Thornton, 2010). The time taken to recover from the crisis was also considerable, after making the market to remain weak for some years, and the market participants to look for a direction, which is by no means straight forward.

Nanto (2009) Opines that the Great Depression and the Global Financial Crisis share some commonalities, not only among them, but also with other financial crises that have occurred in the past. To be specific, the crises are normally associated with the emergence of euphoria accompanied by complacency in the financial markets, which is typically supported by the rapid credit growth followed by a growing that new concepts such as financial innovation or technological advances have rendered old limits of the economic performance to be obsolete. Similarly, Besharove& Douglas (2010) also points out that each crisis has been unique with its own characteristics that make it different from the previous ones.

So as to avoid the next crises, it is inherent to understand the causes and the mechanisms behind the major crisis. Each crisis has its own course in the financial system, and will as a result affect the specific sectors more than others. Looking at the recent major financial crises, the Great Depression of

1930s and the Great Recession of 2008, will provide a clear understanding of the causes and mechanisms behind the financial crises, and therefore, a possibility of coming up with precautionary measure against such a drastic effect as the ones that have resulted from these financial crises.

More importantly, as is the common perception, there are government regulations that follow the crisis. The regulatory bodies also analyze the events to the crises with an aim of bringing down the formal regulations, which would avoid similar crisis in some time to come. After witnessing massive unemployment rates, company bankruptcies, huge losses, the national governments are now pressurized and are also expected to take immediate and concrete actions, that will not only restore market confidence, but also will promise a safe future. However, sometimes the regulatory bodies develop regulations that are not optimal solutions. These regulations can be more than required or sometimes, under the political pressure emphasize on the matters that are not the actual causes of the debacle.

1.2 Understanding the Financial Crisis

Foster (2010) claims that the core problem behind the financial crisis is the peoples belief that the active investments that are provided by the pension funds, mutual funds, banks, hedge funds are all the financial industry have the ability to out-perform the GDP. In accordance to his argument, believing that the financial investment can provide more than the growth of the global portfolio is actually a gross illusion. Similarly, Nanto (2009) states that as long as the future retirees hope for more return, then the world will provide the manure for the development of the species of parasites referred to as the banking and financial industry that feed on the people's illusion and never ending hopes of easy gain. This will continuously lead to emergence of financial crises time from time.

According to Panzer (2008) financial crisis is a situation in which the value of the financial institutions as well as the assets drops drastically. A financial crisis is normally associated with panic along with a run on the banks in which the investors will tend to sell off assets or withdraw money from their savings account with an expectation that the value of the assets will drop when they remain at a financial institution. Nanto (2009) also points out that financial crisis can come as a result of the institutions or assets being overvalued as well as it can be exacerbated by the investor behavior. A rapid string of sell offs will further lead to drop of asset prices or more savings withdrawal. If this situation is left unchecked, then a crisis can cause the economy to progress to a depression or recession.

1.3 Great Depression and Great Recession

The 'Great Depression' came after the 1929 stock market crash and marked the biggest economic crisis that the world had experienced at the time. The depth together with the length of the crisis and the subsequent suffering caused has been legendary. As a result, when he Global Financial Crisis hit in 2007, most believed that the world is about to experience another depression of equal scale and termed it as the Great Recession.

Inherently, capitalism is a system of economic development in which there is a crises feature. There have been many crises occurring even before the 1929 stock market crash as well as after the crash, but the length together with the depth of the great depression has made it a point of locus of refereeing the cruelty of the financial crises. Despite the fact that there has been several debate that tries to establish the causes of the great depression, the late October 1929 New York stock market crash stands out as the defining feature of the crisis. Rothbard (1963) points out that the great depression was the deepest crisis that embraced all disciplines including industrial, social political, financial and even agricultural as well as the longest crisis that also produced catastrophic consequences. Despite the fact that Unites States led the way, great depression was a menace to the rest of the world too. As a result, it the various factors that perpetuated and caused it should be looked.

The 1920s have been referred to as the roaring twenties in America. After the First World War caused significant devastation in the 1910s, 1920 to 1925 was a period where the United States and other international economies experienced a boom. The manufacturing output along with the world mining at the time grew by more than 20 percent. Nevertheless, the gap between the rich and the poor was very high and was still growing bigger. For instance, about four fifths of the United States citizens had no savings as compared to about 24,000 rich families who held more than a third of all the savings. Similarly, during the boom, about 90 percent of the Americans experienced a relative fall in their incomes due to an increase in union-busting and anti-labor laws that resulted to an increase in income inequality. In addition to this, coal mining, textile industries and agriculture was also suffering from the postwar hangover and as expected, the profitability declined and some of the industries wiped out. The inequality concentrated wealth in the hands of very few people and subsequently led to a huge increase in consumer credit. In turn, it sparked off an increase in the private debt levels together with a massive speculative bubble in the form of property boom in Florida.

Between May 1924 and the end of 1925, it was clear that the mania of speculation was not just confined to property, but also there were a significant rise in stock prices of approximately 80 percent. The trend went on and in accordance to Walk (1937), in the early 1928, the boom changed its nature. Basically, there was a mass escape that was aimed at making people believe a part of the speculative orgy. In 1928, the Times Industrials gained a significant 35 percent from 245 points to 331 points. A number of investors then financed their purchase stocks with the borrowed money in order to maximize their gambling profits and the speculators would buy 1000 dollars of stock through putting down 100 dollars. Inherently, the capitalism bubbles have to burst, and this situation was not an exception.

Following this, the United States real economy depicted signs on a slow down even some times before the stock market crashed. Nevertheless, in 23rd October 1929, there was a drop in the stock market that lost almost four months of the former gains and subsequently, the following day people began panic selling (Thornton, 2010). However, this was shortly interrupted by a meeting of the nation's biggest bankers who promised to bring together their resources to stop the slide. The efforts by the banks was however futile since on Black Tuesday October 29th the worst case was experienced and the bottom fell out of the market. This was very serious since it constituted losing all the gains of the previous year. Most of the economists argue that the great depression that resulted lasted for a period of 30 years. The economic impact of the great depression was striking owing to the fact that GNP fell from the peak of $104.4 billion in 1929 to about $56.6 billion in 1933 (Upham and Edwin, 1934). The social impact was also more harrowing since 25 percent of the United States civilian labor force had no jobs by 1933, that is, during the worst point of the depression.

After the recent global financial broke out, a number of people rushed to make comparisons between it and the great depression. However, it also important in this study to make an analysis of the main differences in the nature of the capitalism system between now and the former period. Basically, after the world war boom in output together with the postwar move ito the Keynesian economics that was in a position to save capitalism from self-explosion, there was emergence of neoliberal capitalism in the latter 1970s which came in the form of Thatcherism in Britain and Reaganism in the United States and brought with it a new era of capitalist development different from the previous incarnations distinctly.

The period of the capitalist modification ushered in the creation of an era in which Canterbury was referred to as the casino capitalism. Canterbury (2011) suggests that the era started with three powerful forces coming together. The forces comprised of the monetarism through which Milton Friedman claimed that would bring down inflation with very few effects on production or employment; the neo-Austrians influence which was brought about by the Austrians seeking to reduce the state influence on the entrepreneurs by deregulation; and the pervasive notion that less taxes on the wealthy resulted to trickle-down effect. These policies continued even during the Clinton's era and they gave significant power over the Wall St by deregulation and as a result there was a significant shift from production to financial services. As the financial sector in the United States continued to grow in its asset base, then they became a bigger chunk of the national economy. This was quite evident especially between 1978 and 2005, where the financial sector grew from 3.5 percent to 5.9 percent of the United States economy in accordance to Gross Domestic Product. Inherently, the rate of growth for the financial sector from 1930s to 1980 was almost the same as that of the non-financial sector (Upham and Edwin, 1934). Nevertheless, from 1980 to 2005 the financial sector profitability increases with over 800 percent while the non-financial sector grew with 250 percent. This kind of capitalism, where the profit and value are not practically produced and the result of the speculation is in the form that provides huge power to the unelected rating agencies together with bankers to set the economic agenda which international institutions and governments find difficult to change. It was basically under this system of capitalism that the global financial crisis emerged.

1.4 Gap

The impacts of the Great Depression and Global Financial crises of 2008 have been analyzed. However, the examination of these impacts have been biased on the financial aspect, and therefore, it is also important to look at the social and ecological aspects of the two economic crisis as well. The emergence of the crises have been blamed on the bad behavior on the part of the financial system. In the past century, there has been rapid and substantial social and economic changes all over the world in the wake of globalization. Liberalization has been on high gear and this resulted to a significant decline business and job opportunities. Similarly, structural changes that has been witnessed over the same period has been a catalyst to inflexible labor changes which has resulted to fall in employment along with considerable underutilization of labor (Cochran, 2010). The public health services has also been under immense pressure since the budgets have been squeezed and the market-based reforms also have undermined the resources to investment in public health facilities. Due to the crisis, the local governments also have had to deal with a sharp reduction of their budgets, and they, in turn, have had to reduce their social services. The poverty eradication programs that are supported by the rich nations will also be affected.

The financial crises also put pressure on the existing structures including education. Despite the fact that most of the public schools vary widely across the world, in most countries, they depend directly on government funding for their daily operations. A report by the Amnesty International also shows that the economic crisis did not spare the human rights (Amnesty International, 2009).

Despite all this, the financial systems have always been behaving badly, and therefore, this is not a surprise. Similarly, the crises does not indicate an end to the unwelcome behavior. What, therefore, can we derive from the economic crises to aid us in preparation of any that could be waiting? Financial crises have happened in the past, and will also happen in the time to come. This then rises the question of how prepared we are to a future economic crisis as profound as the Great Recession and Great Depression. Although the examination of these impacts have been biased on the economic point of view, it is, therefore, important to look at the social and ecological aspects of the two economic crisis as well

1.5 Thesis and Theme Justification

The purpose of this thesis paper is to analyze the effects of the two major economic crises, the Great Depression and the Global Financial Crisis of 2008, with a focus on the social and ecological aspects. The paper seeks to understand how society would cope if the economy didn't fully repair itself.

The thesis comes in such a time when the topicality of the recent crisis is overwhelming in the contemporary economic, social and political debates. The financial depression also raised questions regarding the sustainability along with the effectiveness of the neoliberal financial order, which is also a subject in this dissertation. Questions such as why the economic depression have gotten worse, what is the world doing about it and how prepared we are will be ideally answered.

The two crises are a representative case since wide economic and financial recessions have already happened in the past (Bragues, 2009). This is without mentioning the crises throughout the entire financial history that had narrower ranges across the world. This dissertation therefore, contributes to a broader understanding of the nature of the financial crises.

Similarly, it also serves as an exemplary case since the financial crisis may have become a revolutionary event for challenging the deregulated free-market through reinforcing the need for regulation and possible institutions in the global level. Moreover, radical reforms for financial system may lie ahead.

1.6 Methodology and Thesis Structure

The study utilizes a lot of information that is available from various books and scholarly articles on the financial crisis, blogs and newspapers articles, conferences and panel discussions, and websites of central banks together with several regulatory bodies.

In order to comprehend the causes of the two financial crises, it is crucial to understand the past events that led to two crises. This paper hence looks at the pre-crisis environment of the two financial crises by providing a critical comparison of the two economic crises with regard to the factors that led to their emergence. The two great economic crises were largely unexpected. For instance, just before the 2008 crisis, the IMF had announced that risks to the global economy were very low after a careful examination of several economic factors such as the capital inflows, and asset prices. The economic crises can be said to be a product of large credit that comprised of hazardous loans, off-balance sheet operations by the banks, excessive debt leverages, and the inexperience with new financial instruments. The economic crisis will be explained through the theory of neoliberalism.

Consequently, the study, in the third chapter, analyzes the post crises environment of the two economic crises with an aim of establishing whether the problem been efficiently managed. In so doing, the impacts of the crises are analyzed. Actually, the economic crisis has been through several successive stages. The austerity programs have significant negative effects on the labor markets in the world, and has subsequently led to sharply worsening employment outcomes. The employment relations have also become more precarious in the wake of the two financial crises. The jobs became more insecure, uncertain and risky in all the industrial societies. For instance, in United States, the inequality and anxiety that came along with expansion of precarious employment did not only affect how the work was experienced, but also how the households could bear the risks ad also how the society and firms would conduct business. Insecurity, uncertainty, and risk were pervasive within the labor market and have affected the older and younger workers alike.

The overall response to the crises is also examined. This is in regard to the fact that various countries have initiated different response mechanisms that not only aimed at making these countries to stand again on their feet, but also to help them develop shock absorbers in case of such an occurrence. One of the approaches that will be of keen interest is the Lisbon Strategy that is based on the need to increase productivity and competitiveness while enhancing social cohesion in the face of global competition and technology change. One of the schemes launched under this strategy is Europe 2020 that provides recovery guidelines for the EU member states. In addition, other strategies will also be observed.

The study also established the lessons from the two global financial crises. One of crucial issues going forward is how to construct a resilient economic system. There have been numerous crises over the past 200 years despite the fact that the Great depression and GFC were of greater magnitude, and the worst. The emergence of the crises have been blamed on the bad behavior on the part of the financial system. However, the financial systems have always been behaving badly, and therefore, this is not a surprise. Similarly, the crises does not indicate an end to the unwelcome behavior. What, therefore, can we derive from the economic crises to aid us in preparation of any that could be waiting?

In order to understand whether currently the world can cope with another global financial crisis that may arise in the future, the study analyses whether there need for new bodies, in the fourth chapter. The two economic crisis questions the sustainability of our financial, social and ecological systems. This also raises the question of how prepared we are to a third economic crisis. It is therefore, quite clear that there is need to have greater supervision and regulations that should foster countries to develop structures that will help in overcoming such a crisis. The existing structures are analyzed in order to find out the gaps that exist, as well as whether their capability are in question. This will not only cover the economic structures but also the ecological and social structures as well. The chapter will also seek to identify whether there is need to have new institutions in place that would guide recovery process in case of another economic crisis.

Finally, the thesis ends with a conclusion that summarizes the results of the study together with the directions that the paper will consider as important in order to achieve a more desirable social, ecological and economical balance.

1.7 Conclusion

The global financial crises has in the last century been one of the main assaults of the global economic stability to have occurred. It basically describes the regulatory failure in the modern history. The occurrence of the Global Financial Crisis of 2007 -2008 rekindled the memories of a similar financial crisis, the Great Depression, in 1930s. The two financial crises have had profound effects, much more than anticipated by many.

A significant gap on the impacts of the Great Depression and Global Financial crises of 2008 exists since, the examination of these impacts have been biased on the financial aspect, and therefore, it is also important to look at the social and ecological aspects of the two economic crisis as well. Consequently, the purpose of this thesis paper is to analyze the effects of the two major economic crises, the Great Depression and the Global Financial Crisis of 2008, with a focus on the social and ecological aspects. This dissertation therefore, contributes to a broader understanding of the nature of the financial crises. Similarly, it also serves as an exemplary case since the financial crisis may have become a revolutionary event for challenging the deregulated free-market through reinforcing the need for regulation and possible institutions in the global level.

This chapter also highlights the structure and methodology of the dissertation. Specifically, the study utilizes a lot of information that is available from various books and scholarly articles on the financial crisis, blogs and newspapers articles, conferences and panel discussions, and websites of central banks together with several regulatory bodies. The structure comprises of a pre-crisis environment, post-crises environment, and coping with another global financial crisis.

Chapter 2
PRE-CRISES ENVIRONMENT

2.1 Introduction

This chapter will provide a critical comparison of the two economic crises with regard to the factors that led to their emergence. The two great economic crises were largely unexpected. For instance, just before the 2008 crisis, the IMF had announced that risks to the global economy were very low after a careful examination of several economic factors such as the capital inflows, and asset prices. The economic crises can be said to be a product of large credit that comprised of hazardous loans, off-balance sheet operations by the banks, excessive debt leverages, and the inexperience with new financial instruments. The economic crisis will be explained through the theory of neoliberalism. The intent of this dissertation is to analyze the effects of the two major economic crises, the Great Depression and the Global Financial Crisis of 2008, with a focus on the social and ecological aspects. Hans Sennholz (1969) in his article on the Great Depression closed by asking a question, "Can it (Great Depression) happen again? The question though not answered has been answered by the circumstances and time. In the wake of 2008, the stock market experienced another crash that affected the world economy in almost a similar way that the Great depression.

It is undoubtable that the Great Depression was one of the worst economic crisis to have attacked the United States together with other parts of the world. Notably, during the period that led to occurrence of the crisis, there were many fallacious economic policies on the part of the government on a world wide scale. Similarly, United States also underwent a similar period of economic decline that was accented by a crash of the stock market in 2008, The Great Recession. The major financial institutions scrambled for government bailouts. A superficial at the Great Recession points towards the housing babble as the major cause of the economic malaise. When the two great financial crises are examined then it comes out clear that there are significant amount of similarities between the Great Depression and the Great Recession. The similarities of the Great Depression and the Great Recession tends to also indicate that their causes are also similar to each other. It is therefore, the intent of this chapter to look at the pre-crisis factors that contributed to the two crises.

2.2 The Stimulating Resemblances

Inherently, to analyze the Great Depression adequately, then it is crucial to start examining the inflammatory boom that is believed to be behind the stock market crash of 1929. The 1920's was basically characterized by a period of massive business expansion along with production, and this gave it a nick name, "The Roaring 20s". The businesses were booming and so were the income, however, this was also characterized by the roaring inflation that the Federal Reserve had entered into at this particular period. Actually, Johnson (1997) argues that it was this inflation that lead to the emergence of the economic boom in the 1920s. From a layman's perspective, the 1920s cannot be termed as a period of inflation owing to the reason that the prices of commodities remained fairly steady. Inflation is normally associated with rise of prices of goods and services. However, analyzing the situation critically, Keynes (1936) reveals that the industries received mass increase in the production of goods. For example, petroleum production went up by about 12.6 percent, the production of automobiles rose by 4.2 percent annually, the production of manufactured goods increased with about 4 percent while the raw materials also increased with about 2.5 percent. The increase in production lead to subsequent increase in supply, however, the demand remained relatively same. Following the laws of supply and demand, however, the prices of commodities at this period ought to have dropped drastically. Despite this, the inflationary factors of the Federal Reserve Bank forced an upward pressure on the prices of commodities and for this reason, the downward pressure of the increased supply was offset. This resulted to the prices remaining same. At the period, then, it is prudent to claim that inflation can be more associated not with the higher prices instead of prices being higher as it would be the case in a free market. Similarly, it is also worth pointing out that when the numbers are looked at, it is clearer that the money supply in the United States, also rose up significantly with over 55 percent between 1921 and 1929. This can be translated to an average annual rate of 7.3 percent.

Basically, in 1921, a number of European economies were lurching after the end of World War I. similarly, at the same time, the Federal Reserve Bank also entered into a burst of artificial expansion that amounted to over 11.5 billion dollars for a period of five years from 1922. This inflation was aimed at increasing the lending to the foreign government together with banks although Great Britain was the one focus. The lending would subsequently help in stimulating the business activities and production domestically. Foster (2010) notes that the expansion in the bank credit was as a result of three reasons. The first reason is that there was an influx to the United States of around one billion Dollars of gold between 1921 and 1922, secondly, there was a decline of 800 million dollars in money circulation, and finally, the Federal Reserve policies of reducing the rediscount rates as well as increase the holdings of the United States securities. The consequences of the inflation that the Federal Reserve Bank engaged in was not to increase the amount of money in circulation, instead it was to increase the additional loans to the businesses and this resulted to the boom-bust cycle.

After, the crash of the stock market, and the subsequent depression, the only thing that was prudent for the government to do at that time was to step back and watch. Through this way, the economy would have adjusted naturally and also liquidate the malinvestments. Despite this knowledge, Hayek (1933) reveals that the government put pressure on the Federal Reserve Bank to continue inflating in order to stimulate the economy. President Hoover then came up with a program that focused on fixing things by counteracting the view that he was laissez-faire. One of the major programs that was launched by President Hoover was extending emergency loans to the firms that were collapsing and lending to the states so that they can also be in a position to offer relief programs (Panzer, 2008). Hoover also continued to direct the Federal Reserve to continue the path of cheap money, and so the bank lowered the discount rates as well as extended the credit. As a result, this increased the controlled reserves by approximately one billion dollars. Similarly, the Glass Steagall Act was passed by Hoover in 1932 so that it will broaden the eligibility of the assets that can be available for rediscounts with the Fed. The act also allowed the Federal Reserve Bank to utilize the governments bonds as a collateral for the notes and this permitted more inflation and creation of more cheap money (Lee, 1986; Mises, 1983; Rothbard, 1963)

After President Roosevelt took office, he was determined to inflate and also control the nation's money supply more than what Hoover did. However, the United States had a remnant, which presented a small challenge to the president. In order to accomplish his goals, Roosevelt abolished the gold standard through an executive order and commanded that all the citizens to turn in their supplies of gold in exchange of paper dollars. Henninger (2010) argues that Roosevelt actions contributed to an increase in inflation, as it was evident in the increasing reserves along with the continued lowering of the interest rates. Subsequently, this also resulted to more commercial loan being offered which were later to affect the economy again through contributing to another crash in 1937.

Higgs (2006) agrees with the Australian Business Cycle Theory that states if there is an inflationary credit boom that results from the Federal Reserve Bank's lowering of the interest rates, then there will be an enormous misallocation of resource in addition to the capital structure being distorted. With time, all the malinvestments will be realized and the liquidation will also occur but in the form of burst. Considering the Great Depression, the liquidation stage started after the crash of the stock market in 1929. Following this, the Federal Reserve Bank continued to inflate as well as to lower the interest rates through extension of credit and this led to a series of smaller crashes that contributed to the depression, as well as its effects being extended for a long period of time. Moreover, the effects of the additional inflation continued to make that matters worse. Rather than making the economy to adjust naturally, the additional inflation kept bringing down all other efforts to heal the economy and for this reason, then prolonging the downturn with intrusive policies. This continued inflation policies were contrary to the lesson learned following the 1929 depression.

A similar mechanism was seen during the period that led to the 2008 financial crisis along with the subsequent stock market crash. Most of the procedures by the Federal Reserve Bank have been repeated. The housing Bubble that is believed to be the cause of the Great Recession was formed majorly through inflation together with the government backed securities. Consequently, there were also significant misallocation of the resources in the housing market which also led to pilling up of the malinvestments. The malinvestments came evident as people started to default loans and the crisis also rapidly sped through the financial sector before affecting the rest of the economy. Just like the factors that resulted to the Great Depression, inflation was at the heart of the factors especially after the Federal Reserve Bank pumped banks full of reserves in order to dish out mortgage loans. Similarly, the terrorist attack in September 11, 2001, made Alan Greenspan to direct the Federal Reserve to lower their discount rates to one percent (Bragues, 2009; Dorning, 2011; Folsom, 2008). As a result, the lifespan between 200o and 2007, there were more creation of dollars which amounted to over 214 billion dollars which was the largest creation of dollars ever in the history of United States. Each time the Federal Reserve Bank lowers the interest rate through increasing the supply of money, it tends to encourage production in longer-tem projects. In the case of the 2008 financial crisis, there was a boom in the house construction. In addition to this, banks were also in a position to increase the number of mortgages that they had loaned out, although this was the other goal of Federal Reserve Bank. Despite the fact that a number of analysts place emphasis on the subprime loans, it is also crucial to note that the foreclosures occurred at a similar time for both the subprime and the prime markets. As a result, it may not be that prudent to blame the subprime market as the one that affected the prime loan market, as many contemporaries do, however, the two markets were largely affected by the significant increase of credit (Besharove& Douglas 2010; Bragues, 2009; Cochran, 2010). Actually, the Federal Reserve Bank together with their inflationary procedures should be blamed for creating the housing possible and as a result leading to an unnatural increase in the housing prices (Dorning, 2011; Dubay, 2011;Folsom, 2008). Just like the Great Depressions, the controversies revolving around inflation were not realized with stock market crash and there Federal Reserve Bank continued to harm the economy more and more through its inflationary procedures after the crisis hit.

Redundant Spending

The main focus for the US and many other nations has been determining the relationship between financing the US federal government, and the degree at which the taxes and debts affect the entire economy of the US. The spending allocated for federal government is a question subject to discussions and is the main focus of the government, and which most politicians are turned to. The analysis has shown that there are two important aspects that should be looked upon and taken care of, in order to understand how taxation and inflation affects the entire budgeting and funding of the federal government

(Wheelock, 1992). The first aspect is focused on how the government spending economically twists the federal government economy. The second school of thought seeks to understand how deficit spending affects implementation of the federal government economic expenditures (Lonto, 2011). Comparing the two aspects selects deficit spending as having inflicting impacts on the economy. Understanding this aspect requires understanding of other related and close complexities, and hindrances that altogether affects economic growth. From first principles, government spending of any type includes transferring of national resources from private or individual producers to selected users as wished by the political government officials. Some economists argue that government spending is somehow investment but still, some tend to view the government spending as being consumptive in nature. Typically, government spending cannot be ascertained as being investment because, investment is whereby investors or entrepreneurs allocates some resources that would otherwise have been spend on consumption, and directs the saved resources towards increasing the production. By producing more resources, capital is created and therefore government spending is consumptive and not investment (Lonto, 2011).

In many case scenarios, government spending has a tradition of transferring funds from noted profitable enterprise or manufacturing companies, while at the same time subsidizing the less performing or less profitable enterprises (Wheelock, 1992). This approach and methodologies applied by the government pro officials ensures that the less profitable companies or businesses are prolonged far from failing and are prevented from performing below the targeted levels. The main intention of the government spending through enterprises ensures that small business enterprises are propped up to perform better in a competitive government environment. Fundamentally, all enterprises are important and their services are necessary though the free market has in most economic scenarios failed to avail them. The free market does not support or sustain small enterprises because either the businesses are unprofitable, unreliable or mostly, inefficient. However if these featured goods and services are of great benefit or necessary to the society, then the entrepreneurs would decide better to either produce goods or services at any given time. The description outlined therefore reveals that the government would always try to perpetuate unsuccessful, losing or market inefficiencies (Wheelock, 1992).

Applying the same government analytical principles reveals that spending being consumptive is closely associated with government borrowing and government spending. Economists have therefore revealed that there is a big financial gap with regard to loans. When an individual borrows a loan from a bank, the loans is used to further the production, which ends up generating great profits within good time. Some percentage of the profits is used to pay off the accumulated private or individual debts (Wheelock, 1992). In contrast, government borrowing scenario is opposite because when the same occurrence occurs, the government avails more resources and hand supplies of necessary avenues which encourages the government politicians to spend. The spending freedom opened to the politicians encourages them to overspend, because they have the mandate of deciding where to channel the resources. This scenario increases level of consumption and it even puts extra strain and drain on capital employed. This is because the employed capital is not streamlined to produce extra resources, goods and services that may be used to pay off the borrowed money (Wheelock, 1992). The nature of borrowing is also significant because the avenue through which the government borrows money has a significant impact at the end of each stage of resources allocation. There are many avenues through the government can gain money or borrow money from other sources. If the government borrows from within its jurisdiction, domestically or locally, the market will be in chaos because the entrepreneurs will have no money to invest and increase production. Lack of market stability therefore exists when the government borrows high amounts of money from within (Lonto, 2011). The market has also been known to get crowded with economic nightmares among the entrepreneurs because they cannot get enough finances to boost their investments. Economic analysis has also pointed out that when nations or a selective government borrows from a different nation or foreign country, the market total exports starts to decline with time because the creditors being the lenders switches off from buying goods from indebted nation and instead, they commence buying bonds in large quantities from indebted country. As a result, a government continuingly increases its debt with time, and it may do so until the entire production stage is sabotaged or made tight for entrepreneurs to maneuver economically. Few but notable steps have been noted by the economists as being the avenue through which they respond when the amount of debt increases considerably (Lonto, 2011). Key noted responses is that, the government may decide to do curtail spending, raise taxes for its citizens to raise enough amount to pay off the debt. The last response is that the government may decide to increase inflation or sometimes may combine the inflation and the taxing to work simultaneously. The worst happens when the government overtaxes its citizens because it only creates more trouble and instabilities in the market environment.

The government of the United States experienced a decreased spending in most of the 1920s period only to rise later slowly at the end of the 1920-decade when the stock market became stable and when the stock market enormous crash approached. The documentation made at this time, together with the information kept indicates that the debt also decreased. Later own, the depression period started, leading to increased government spending and increase in total deficits. This scenario came into light when the president of the United States, Roosevelt met and discussed in detail with John Maynard, economist. Maynard suggested that the government increases vast expenditures in combination with monetary expansion. The economist advocated for this approach because he thought the blended strategies could increase profits for the government. In response, Roosevelt announced publicly about his new government spending program in January 1934, contrarily to procedures which required him to announce the spending program in December 1933. While making his new announcements, he made a public promise that the deficit could reduce to $7 billion shillings, and which he announced to be settled in a period of six months. In the last eleven years, before this announcement was made by the president, the entire federal government had spent a total of $4.52 billion (Lonto, 2011). This amount divided by eleven months mutually or uniformly shows that the average monthly expenditure stood at $410 million. The expenditure by Roosevelt for the month of November, December 1933, and January 1934 increased considerably from $505 million, $703 million, and $956 million respectively. The increase in the spending program came after he made his announcement. The increase in the governmental expenditure led to a deficit amounting to $4billion in a period of six months, but which came slightly below the targeted figure of $7billion shillings. Following his superfluous expenditure,

Roosevelt requested the congress to give him more money to spend on his alleged plan of expanding the job market. Following his request, Roosevelt was allocated a check of $4.880 billion to spend as he wished. Roosevelt combined analytical accounting skills to put together a bill that accumulated to $13.6 billion of the total allotted $4.88 billion. Enclosed in the bill was a planned stage of planting trees between the Mexico and Canada, but a plan, which was prohibited by the agricultural appropriation act. This was enough for Roosevelt to spend money in a superfluous way and is documented that by end of 1937, Roosevelt had spend a total of $7756 billion (Lonto, 2011).

The most significant difference between the two notable periods is solely based on the bailing out of firms. Economists and political economists have identified that Hoover's time ended with one of the most remarkable results with regard to ending of the inflation, and that the major role and goal of this time was closely related to bailing out of various business and enterprises. However, the most recent changes are economical and sustainable on the government side because it has established an ante which has ended up the ante towards bailing out some of the most notable distressed or poorly performing companies and or business enterprises. Good examples still exists where by the federal government at one point decided to buy out the Bear Stearns company which after some significant time, was handed over to the JB Morgan, a company that has quite for sometime been managing lots of businesses. The same federal government at a later date, decided to hand over a bail out of about $85 billion to AIG Company. During the same year, the federal government handed over bailouts to three automakers, with highly influential services in the markets. Despite offer of the bailouts, the companies were not performing any better, a scenario that created the necessity of enacting a new act that could at least uplift the company from their lowest levels of performance. As a result, the federal government congress established an emergency economic act in 2008 in order to stabilize the performance of the companies. By doing this, the federal government was authorizing the governmental treasury of the US to purchase about $700 billion of some specified and several assets. To some economists, this was a repetition of the former process by this time, through a legal agreed upon act of 2008. The main shock came in when after the government had bought the assets, it later on sold the assets at a notable and devastating loss. Despite this, the federal government once again bought assets amounting to $700 billion, and after which they again sold them at a big notable loss. During the same time, there was a notable establishment of another program, which allowed the treasury to seize any type of financial institution operating within the US jurisdiction without any further instruction or outlining the procedures on how the same could be done. The treasury was also given mandate of seizing the operational financial institutions at any sort of price the treasury may think off. The program was called Troubled Assets relief based program and was initialized as TARP. The results after this development was so loose and devastating because the treasury launched several unidirectional mode and way of buying several sprees anonymously, a scenario that led to serious inflation that that changed the market condition within a very short period of time (Lonto, 2011).

Economist and politicians have identified that there are various divergences between great recession and great depression. However, monetary inflation is one of the main reasons that is used to indicate the divergences. However, the two periods of times had similar problems related to each other and still the two periods had similar events such as increased taxation. The taxation talked about has similar characteristics existing inform of progressive based income taxation. The most notable characteristics of the great depression is that, when president Franklin took office, he became more of a proponent than an antagonist. His major will was to restore the prosperity of the U.S. The time he took over the office, the Great Depression period was in its middle times. However, the will and actions he took thereafter only reflected characteristics of the opposite period. It turned out that his wish and will was closely associated with redistribution of the U.S wealth to all races and people, but he failed to factor in the element of increasing the revenues of the U.S (Thornton, 2010).

The same concentration of ideas outlines that in 1933, the US president of the US by then, Roosevelt had engineered all actions towards improving the economy of the US even though the results of the actions were not good according to what was evidenced in 1933. The income based taxation rates was recorded o be highest in 1934 following the actions that were conducted and applied by the congress under the leadership of President Roosevelt. The taxation rates ranged from 13.5% to about 69.9% on those who were earning $20,000 and $5,000,000 a year or more respectively. The rates were also increased when in 1935, the president tried to circumvent the then US based constitution by saying that all bills collected on taxes should originate from House of Representatives (Thornton, 2010). This approach meant to attach the identified rider on a senate bill, which ended up raising the tax rates. During this time of proposal, the citizens together with politicians lamented and got infuriated about the steps that the president had taken. As a result, the rider was shot down but the president together with the congress decided to propose a new bill that contained different patterns but which reflected features of the former rider's proposal. The bill proposed by Roosevelt was noted and identified as H.R 8974. The congress agreed to pass the bill, and after passing, the rates on taxes increased from the former 13.5% to 13.9% for those who were making accumulative $20,000 in a year and rocketed to 83.2% for those who were making about % 4,000,000 in a year or more. It was realized that when the rate of taxation was increased, the burden is left to the citizen who is a tax payer at all times, and therefore, when the burden increases through excessive taxation, the tax payer has to yield or respond by reducing expenses on lifestyle and better lives in order to pay the taxes to the government (Lonto, 2011). Many politicians have also argued that, lives of people and citizens become very difficult to maneuver and exist in a tax strained nation and therefore the live standards reduce considerably. All the worst conditions indicate that when taxation when working with the government becomes worse, many citizens start to opt working for leisure than within the government portfolios or frameworks. Shifting from work to leisure widens the economic downturn gap, leading to increased poverty among societies and government. The turmoil experienced for this group points out that it is sometimes good to work for nonmonetary rewards rather than to work for monetary rewards, which are highly taxed (Thornton, 2010). For the recession and depression period, there was lack of specialization because many people or citizens preferred working from their homes rather than working for the government. The result is fatal because the labor market breaks down, and as such, the economic development is reversed considerably. While the labor market reduces, regression increases within families, but with a corresponding increase in taxation rates (Lonto, 2011). The question which remains is why should the government overtax individuals who have increased their production efficiently towards creation of jobs and increasing of revenues for the country?. Some economist argue that reducing taxes will obviously avail great money for the government, and still, the living standards will increase, leading to a healthy community that has strength and energy to work towards producing better services and goods. For the scenario which occurred during great depression, progressive taxes ended up paralyzing the efforts and economic moves of the richest people in the nation because their gap and freedom to invest was highly noted and followed closely by the government taxing watch dog (Rothbard, 1963).

The results of the progressive income taxation was the worsening of the economic condition in the market, a condition which only required some incentives or little incentives to uplift the motivation among the richest people to work better towards improving the economic condition or bringing up level of revenues. Similarly, progressive income based taxation was notable in great recession period with a slight difference such that it was not economically penal compared to the great depression. However, a clear description of the past trend shows that the U.S tax trends and brackets for the last decade shows that the tax brackets have somehow remained steady and average. The same analysis points at Obama, the current president who is constantly and slowly stepping into Roosevelt's shoes. Despite several changes, the president is succumbing into great depression, and is continuously proposing indirectly the issue of progressive taxation on entrepreneurs (Thornton, 2010). He has been proposing increases in progressive taxation, a scenario that is economically crippling the economic development of the U.S. When the president Obama first took office, the Bust cut tax effect was still in place and was to end in January of 2011.

However, Obama strategically and persistently urged the existing congress to allow for the tax cuts to end instantaneously in order to pave way for his manifesto to take effect.

When the congress immediately allowed for the changes, the state of the economy and of the U.S returned to 2001 scenario, which is characterized with presentation of high rates of taxation on governmentally employed people, and entrepreneurs operating within the U.S jurisdiction. In addition, Obama called for an average of $921 billion increases in tax, and which was to take effect from first day of January, 2011 (Lonto, 2011). By doing this, the tax burden was drastically increased from low levels to significantly levels. The overburden scenario signifies that most people will start to prefer working during their leisure times than working for the government, and also working better under different ownership or environment rather than the government (Rothbard, 1963). The worst trend is that, most of people will become poor, and the living standards for most people will drastically reduce (Thornton, 2010). Despite the levels of globalization, most people will have to suffer great losses due to over taxation, and due to poor market condition for investors (Rothbard, 1963). The actions taken by president Obama at that time did not work very well, and allover a sudden, the U.S was in inflation, and the value of the dollar reduced considerably. The recession of 2008 is considered one of the results of his actions while in office. To combat this situation, the government strategically looked for some options. Buffet's rule also outlines that richest men should be taxed more compared to middle income citizens who have extra burden to bear.

2.3 Outstanding Obliviousness

Every blame has been directed at men who either discussed future of the country with the president. However, the blame extents to citizens who elect the congressmen and women to represent them economically, and politically. The congressman and women give comments that reflect their experiences and backgrounds while in college, and therefore much blame for the both depression and recession is closely related to the teaching availed in colleges and universities by scholars. Some of the key scholarly influences is seen in increased labor wage laws, farming laws, and length of protective tariffs (Lonto, 2011). Great depression was strongly sawn by intellectuals or institutional scholars who always advocated for enactment of protective and wage laws. During the 1929 period, everyone was hoping for the better in economy and little consequences were expected to come out of inflation except the Austrians who expected that there could be challenges and breakdowns in stock markets. One of the most notable economists was the Austrian economist called Ludwig von who contradicted with Fisher that crash in bond and stock was strongly inevitable. However at this time of depression, Ludwig was considered a doom economic prophet and therefore an upper hand was given to Fisher who consistently gave hope of better economic development. However, the trend worsened, and the crash was evidenced in 1929 (Rothbard, 1963). In addition, Paulson Henry from the financial treasury of the US had assured people that everything was fine and that there was nothing different from what he had seen while pursuing in his career. However the crash only came seven months later, confirming that he had misled minds of people and deviated their knowledge about the same.

2.4 Conclusion

When the two great financial crises are examined then it comes out clear that there are significant amount of similarities between the Great Depression and the Great Recession. The similarities of the Great Depression and the Great Recession tends to also indicate that their causes are also similar to each other. The Great depreciation and the Great Recession was both challenging to societies and to American entrepreneurs because it was associated with rise in taxation rates and inflation rates of the highest order that could be notable in the entire world. A scrutiny of the same reveals that congress influenced by the scholarly education and institutional experiences was the major cause of most financial or economic turmoil because of the ideologies taught at the colleges and universities. The ideologies that are currently available in literature is quite trick to understand and to apply because it contains elements of individual and or personal understanding of the statement. Depression is at the sides and if conducive room is created, it comes into effect with full features that can challenge existence of human beings or human beings in any nation. Taxation avails a trick burden to citizens who may at any time devise methods of survival, and which may challenge implementation of the existence of a stable or progressive market of any country. Politicians are to be blamed for all the changes and without the consideration of scholars at the institutions; the nation is much more unstable. Our societies are shaped by moral standards, and traditions. As such, any change or proposal for change brought forward for change must be included must be considered as having social and political flaws, but within manageable or sustainable levels. The citizens should expect that the political and economical cycle repeats itself and therefore, there must be reforms, and strategies to cope with the market environments when such cycles tends to repeat themselves.

Chapter 3
POST CRISES ENVIRONMENT: HAS THE PROBLEM BEEN EFFICIENTLY MANAGED?

3.1 Introduction

In the past two decades, there have been rapid and substantial social and economic changes all over the world in the wake of globalization. Liberalization has been on high gear and this resulted to a significant decline business and job opportunities. Similarly, structural changes that has been witnessed over the same period has been a catalyst to inflexible labor changes which has resulted to fall in employment along with considerable underutilization of labor. According to Calomiris, (2008), the underlying overall impact of the financial crises did not only have profound effects on the world's economy but also on the households across the world.

The economic crisis has been through several successive stages. The austerity programs have significant negative effects on the labor markets in the world, and have subsequently led to sharply worsening employment outcomes. The employment relations have also become more precarious in the wake of the two financial crises. The jobs became more insecure, uncertain and risky in all the industrial societies. For instance, in United States, the inequality and anxiety that came along with expansion of precarious employment did not only affect how the work was experienced, but also how the households could bear the risks ad also how the society and firms would conduct business. Insecurity, uncertainty, and risk were pervasive within the labor market and have affected the older and younger workers alike. Various countries have initiated different response mechanisms that not only aimed at making these countries to stand again on their feet, but also to help them develop shock absorbers in case of such an occurrence. One of crucial issues going forward is how to construct a resilient economic system. There have been numerous crises over the past 200 years despite the fact that the Great depression and GFC were of greater magnitude, and the worst. The emergence of the crises have been blamed on the bad behavior on the part of the financial system. However, the financial systems have always been behaving badly, and therefore, this is not a surprise. Major lessons have then been withdrawn from these crises. In this chapter, the impact, response and lessons from the crises will be analyzed.

3.2 The impacts of the Crises

Claessens, Ayhan and Marco (2008), argues that the Great Recession cannot be blamed wholly for the precarious work. Technological change, globalization, re-regulation of the labor markets as well as the removal of the institutional protections have been shifting the balance of power away from the workers and towards the employers. As a result, this has made the precarious work to be increasingly common across the world. The shift in the power relations can generally be referred to as the structural transformations in the labor market. Romer (2009) supports the argument by noting that the growth in the precarious employment occurred after majority of countries abandoned the implicit social contract that would bind the government, labor, and business together for a number of years after the Second World War. Similarly, Reinhart and Kenneth (2009) points out that labor market conditions after the Great Recession had deteriorated dramatically making it the severest labor market downturn since the 1930s depression. In United States, the unemployment rate rose from 4.8 percent in 2007 to 10 percent in 2009. The convectional unemployment understates the labor market distress and misses the huge growth in the underemployment as well as a substantial increase in the discouraged workers. The payroll employment similarly recorded a significant decline of approximately 6.1 percent from 2007 to 2010. However, the labor market started to recover modestly in March 2010, with a promise of 160 thousand jobs. Similar situation was also reflected in other countries as well. In Europe, the unemployment rates also increased significantly (Huizinga and Luc, 2009).

The unemployment increases in the Great Recession affected workers disproportionately. The downturn was severe to a point that it had adverse effects on all the groups of workers and all regions across the world in terms of stagnant wages and substantial unemployment.

According to Reinhart and Kenneth (2009) the labor market deterioration from 2007 to 2009, after the Great Recession was accompanied by a historical cyclical negative relationship between job openings or vacancies and unemployment. In United States, the rising unemployment in 2009 seemed to be severe although the normal cyclical unemployment increased. The unemployment rate continued to increase in 2009 even after the job openings rate had stabilized and the unemployment rate became higher than it would have been implied by the historical Beveridge curve (Arellano,

Bai and Kehoe, 2010). This pattern implies that the emergence of structural unemployment problems of mismatches between the unemployed together with potential new jobs along with exacerbation of the longer-term labor market trends in different countries of the rising wage inequalities together with the decline in the employment opportunities in the traditional middle-class jobs.

Despite the fact that the historical Beveridge curve depicted an apparent outward shift that showed some increase in the structural labor market issues, it is clear that there is still a huge cyclical unemployment problem with a continued severe shortfall of the aggregate demand along with the real GDP is also below the potential trend level. The rise of the long-term unemployment shows cyclical collapse of the aggregate demand along with the labor demand. The hiring rates remained low for a big period of time, and the job losers together with labor market new entrants and reentrants found it difficult to find work quickly as well as have much greater risk of becoming long-term unemployed. The Job opening vacancy rate in Europe declined from 3.2 percent in 2007 to 1.8 in 2009, and then stabilized in 2010 at 2.1 percent rate.

Mason (2009) reports that the decline in the employment tenure occurred just as internal labor markets weakened. This was evident through the increasing tendency for the employers to hire workers from outside the organization instead of developing the human capital internally.in addition, the trends in the involuntary job loss shows that job stability along with insecurity have been declining since 1970s

A key component of policies were formulated in order to assist the long-term unemployed people together with their families, which comprised of the continuation of extended unemployment insurance benefits in United States. Huizinga and Luc (2009) argue that the disincentive effects of the unemployment insurance extensions contributed to the rising long-term unemployment as well. On the other hand, Reinhart and Kenneth (2009) points out that only modest impacts of the unemployment insurance extensions could be felt during the search effort and duration of the unemployment of the unemployment insurance recipients.

The dramatic cyclical downturn of the Great Recession came in after a period of increase of wage inequality and educational wage differentials in Europe and United States (Ohanian and Raso, 2012). The large rise in the wage inequality has been related to the rapid skill biased technological change that is associated with the computerization or globalization. For instance, in 1990s to 2007, there was a finance boom that had aspects of globalization and off shoring and as a result weakening the labor market institutions. This led to exacerbated wage inequality trends. The last two decades have seen United States labor market become polarized due to twisting of technological change along with the rise in the offshoring. The polarization was evidenced by strong growth in the high-end, high skill jobs and in the traditionally lower wage jobs although with weak demand for the traditional middle class jobs like manufacturing production jobs along with middle management positions. The housing market boom along with the bubble of 2002 to 2006 hid these trends in the buoying demand for the non-college men in the construction. Nevertheless, the Great Recession reinforced the long-term jobs polarization together with wage inequality trends as well as declines in manufacturing, construction and middle management employment.

The long-term structural labor market issues shows that there is a significant mismatch between the aspiration of a job losers and skills. The skill requirements along with compensation packages of new job openings are likely to emerge as the economy recovers from the Great Recession. Most of the Job losers from different sectors such as manufacturing and construction, however, may face difficulties in making the financial and psychological adjustments along with gaining the education and training required for the new jobs available for the growing primary sectors.

The social problems have also deepened resulting to a deterioration of the quality of life. Crimes rate also tends to increase during the hard times. For instance, crime increased during certain expansionary periods in 1960s as well as between 2007 and 2010. Additionally, there has been an increased pressure on the education services, as a result, it has become more difficult to provide the labor market with the needed skills.

According to Reinhart and Kenneth (2009) the trends in poverty and social inclusion in Europe using the indicators provided by the NSI as based on the European Survey on the living conditions and income. The poverty line is defined by the monetary indicator that is used to identify the poor in the society. In the European survey, the poverty line was set at 60 percent of the average total disposable net income per equivalent unit. The survey used EUR 150.8 average per person as the poverty line, which revealed that about 20.7 percent of the people in Europe lived below the poverty line.

Huizinga and Luc (2009) reveal that the policies regarding poverty and social exclusion have given significant attention to the working poor phenomenon currently. The working poor include the people who work, and secondly are still members of poor households. As such the definition of the working poor depends on two units. First, the single individual, and secondly the household. The individual marks the beginning of classification of the unemployed ad employed while the household provides the basis for the classification of either poor or non-poor. In accordance this, there are some individuals who live in poor households and their income is clearly above the poverty line. Also there are other groups of people whose individual income are well below the threshold and still live in poor households. According to Liu, Wang and Zha (2011), in 2007 to 2009, there were over 7 percent of the employed people who lived in the households that had an income that is below the poverty line in Europe. Moreover, Herkenhos, and Ohanian, (2012a) also states that the risk of poverty for the individuals who were working part-time in 2005 was greater than for those working full-time. This revelation is an indicator of the unfavorable position the part-time employees in the labor market during the recession found themselves in.

Manuelli and Peralta-Alva (2011) argues that an individual's level of education plays a crucial role in determination of better paid jobs, and it is directly related to the poverty levels among the employed people. For the workers who had lower-secondary education, their share of the poor in 2009 increased by 3.8 percent as compared to 2008, which was 26.5 percent. On the other hand, the share of the poor for the other education groups such as level 3, 4, and 5, 6, was not affected by the negative effects of the global crisis in 2009.

Huizinga and Luc (2009) argues that in relation to the goals that were established in the Europe 2020 strategy, a combined indicator to be used in monitoring the individual countries progress in achieving their national targets can be estimated by looking and the income and living conditions in the respective countries. One of the indicators used in monitoring is the at-risk-poverty rate, the rate of people living in households with low work intensity and the severe material deprivation rate. When the indicators are combined together, it is clear that in 2009 almost half of the population in Europe were in need of special care in order to overcome social inequality and exclusion from active work. Actually, Keane and Rogerson (2012) reveals that the negative trend with respect to the share of the population at risk or social exclusion began in 2008, and in the following year, there was a dramatic increase resulting from the economic downturn with more than two times from 1.4 percentage points in 2008 to 3.0 percent in 2009. Herkenhos and Ohanian (2012b) also notes that the situation of men was more affected by the financial crisis since in 2009, the share of men at risk of the social exclusion or poverty increased by 3.2 percent while for women only increased by 2.8 percent. In comparison with the 2007, when the figures were 1.1 and 1.7 percent, it is well clear that the industrials sector where mainly men provide the labor force suffered more from the effects of recession and this in turn reduced demand and also led to production cuts along with mass lay-offs.

Eggertsson (2008) notes that in poorer countries, poverty cannot be entirely blamed on an individual but rather it is as a result of a combination of several factors such as personal, national, regional, and also international influences. There is normally little in the way to help the people who are not to blame for their predicament. Despite the fact that there are some wonderful strategies aimed at addressing global poverty, for instance the millennium Development Goals, the threat of the effects of the financial crisis may not spare such. For example, the Great Recession, by itself affected these strategies, which are normally funded by the international bodies, such that the funds that was available to achieve the goals was greatly reduced. Although this is better than nothing, it shows that most of the leading nations may lack political will to continue as well as aim for more ambitious targets to eradicate poverty in the third world countries. Nevertheless, they could be as well be willing to find more save in their own banks.

Notably, the poorer nations normally get aid from the richer nations, and it was not expected that during the financial crisis, that also affects the rich nations, they would be in a position to support the poor nations. As a result, the poverty eradication programs that are supported by the rich nations will also be affected. According to Kehoe, Ruhl and Steinberg (2012) the issue of tax haven is also crucial for the poor countries. The Tax havens normally result in the moving of capital from the poor countries into havens. A crucial source of revenue is normally the domestic tax revenues which contributes about 13 percent of the low income countries earnings, and on the other hand, it accounts for 36 percent for the rich countries (Garriga, Manuelli, and Peralta-Alva, 2012). The United Nations sponsored conference in November 2008 that was aimed at addressing the issue, was not very successful thanks to the recession fears along with the financial crisis. According to Leamer (2007) the estimated capital flight cost the poor countries approximately 500 billion dollars in lost revenue. This definitely outweighed the foreign aid with a factor of 5. The lost tax revenue is very crucial to the poor countries. This is because it could help in paying debts, and also reduce or eliminate the need for depending on the foreign aid or even be used by the poor countries to help them become more independent from the influence of the rich nations.

The financial crises also put pressure on the existing structures including education. Despite the fact that most of the public schools vary widely across the world, in most countries, they depend directly on government funding for their daily operations. In United States, the primary method of funding the public schools is through tax from the federal government, but the state government normally source their funding from alcohol and cigarette, and motor vehicles exercise taxes along with more specialized taxes and other sources like the mineral leases and lottery. The sources of funding for education in United States took a hit during the recession. Although the sales tax receipts as well as the personal income tax receipts grew steadily from 2000 to 2008, the fell significantly in 2009 by 2.41 percent and by 6.33 percent in 2010. Similar case was also observed in other taxes (Garriga, Manuelli, and Peralta-Alva, 2012). With a decrease in the total tax collected after the recession, the funding of the public schools was also negatively affected. Basically, there was a clear decline of funding.

A report by the Amnesty International also shows that the economic crisis did not spare the human rights. Inherently, the human rights have been of concern for a long time. The recent years have seen the increasing acknowledgement that the human rights together with the economic issues like development are interrelated. According to Kocherlakota (2012), before the financial crisis took hold, the human rights concern were on high gear, in accordance to the human rights organisations such as Amnesty International annual reports. However, with the global financial crisis that resulted to an economic crisis, there was a turn around that also ended up in human rights crisis too. Amnesty International 2009 annual report shows that as millions slide into poverty due to the financial crisis, the social unrest also tends to increase and it is characterized by more protests. These protests are most of the times met with suppression while other times, people will be exploited further.

This notion is also supported by the World Bank, which forewarned of a human catastrophe in the world's poorest countries if nothing will be done in order to tackle the global economic crisis. Moreover, Landvoight (2011) also had anticipated massive social upheaval if there was nothing done about the crisis. After the G20 summit in 2009, there were significant reports from the media about the excessive force used by the police against the protesters that even resulted to death of passerby who was mistaken for a protester. According to Kehoe, Ruhl and Steinberg (2012) many nations witnessed protests against economic decline together with social conditions, which were met with violence, arrests along with detentions without charge. This was a clear violation of human rights that could be termed as a negative effect of the global financial crisis.

"Across Africa, people demonstrated against desperate social and economic situations and sharp rises in living costs. … Some demonstrations turned violent; the authorities often repressed protests with excessive force.

Social tensions and economic disparities led to thousands of protests throughout China. In the Americas, social protest at economic conditions increased in Peru; in Chile there were demonstrations throughout 2008 on Indigenous People's rights and rising living costs." Amnesty International (May 28, 2009).

The public health services has also been under immense pressure since the budgets have been squeezed and the market-based reforms also have undermined the resources to investment in public health facilities.

In a number of countries the local governments have been overburdened with more responsibilities due to such policies as decentralization, which in some countries like Kosovo, Bosnia, Herzegovina, and Macedonia have come up with support programs for the ethnic conflicts.

Nevertheless, with the due to the crisis, the local governments have had to deal with a sharp reduction of their budgets, and they, in turn, have had to reduce their social services.

3.3 The overall Response to the Crises

Various countries have initiated different response mechanisms that not only aimed at making these countries to stand again on their feet, but also to help them develop shock absorbers in case of such an occurrence. One of the approaches that have been of keen interest is the Lisbon Strategy that is based on the need to increase productivity and competitiveness while enhancing social cohesion in the face of global competition and technology change.

3.3.1 Policies

One of the schemes launched under this strategy is Europe 2020 that provides recovery guidelines for the EU member states. In addition, other strategies will also be observed. The European integration deepened further as evidenced since 1990, and the leadership of the European Union (EU) countries has been setting grandiose politico-economic landmarks. In 1990s, there was "Agenda 2000: For a stronger and wider Union" which aimed at reinforcing its policies together with accession of new member states, and then there was the "Lisbon Strategy" in 2000s which focused on setting the Union to become the most competitive and dynamic knowledge based economy in the world. After the recession, the Union introduced the Agenda 2020. Agenda 2020 seeks proper policies that can strengthen the Union's political and economic power and as a result help it to achieve a prominent role in the 21st century globalized environment while at the same time retain the social cohesion together with high-level of the living standards along with the economic convergence among the member states.

Inherently, the recent financial crisis affected major economies, which comprised of Italy, United Kingdom, Germany, Italy among others, and had seriously jeorpadized the EU convergence procedure as well as raised serious doubts concerning the financial viability of the welfare state. At the same time, there was deterioration of social indicators in the continent. The EU's inclusive arm also has been shaken through increased unsustainable distribution of income, and as a result, this erode the social security destroying the significant social achievements of the industrialized countries including their capacity to guarantee a reasonable income to the citizens who were hit by the unfavorable conditions. In addition, there was also significant decrease of the public and private investments along with the rate of employment among the young people, which resulted to unfavorable effects on the development prospects because the growing part of the European societies has been pushing out for labor market. This in turn retains the consumption together with entrepreneurial prospects in low levels. Notably, the issue of unemployment remained unresolved with regard to the European employment strategy and was not to be of concern, however, it is core for the European economies especially because Italy, Germany, and France has been exposed to long-term unemployment rates. The high rates demanded to new strategies because restoring full employment is synonymous to preventing long-term unemployment. This and other issues have been set as priorities and targets that are set in the Europe 2020 agenda. Specifically, the agenda aims at resolving issues concerning employment, climate change and energy sustainability, research and development, education, poverty, and social inclusion. The agenda also seeks to reposition Europe after financial crisis.

Similarly, the United States policy making during the Great Recession seems to be a reaction of the events of the 1930s, as well as efforts to avoid a severe meltdown as the one resulted from the Great depression. Sullivan (1951) reports that the lessons from Great Depression comprises of disentangling those that have already been learned from the ones that remain outstanding. It is therefore crucial to note that the modern central banking together with monetary theory were progressing in 1930s. As a result, much learning occurred during the Great depression itself (Temin, 1989; Walk, 1937; Wigmore, 1985). Consequently, exiting the financial crisis called for recovery that comprised reversals from the historic central banking policies with an aim of maintaining the gold parity standards.

The crucial policy shocks in the history of the central banking comprise of the open market sales by the Federal Bank at the beginning of 1928 to 1929, the changes in the discount rate, at 1929. These two policies were aimed at dampening the shock market speculation.

According to Agnew (1945), the monetary policy mistakes contributed to the crisis in the United States economy in the 1930s, and since the Federal bank was constrained by their adherence to the gold standard, it was practically hard for them to prevent banks from failing. Similarly, growth also stopped in 1937-38 because of the policy mistake of the Federal bank, specifically, by doubling the reserve requirements between 1936 and 1937. This made the banks to lend even less than they had previously.

The rescue operations by the Federal Bank for the Great Recession began in March 2008. The financial markets at the time had been unusually strained and the Federal Reserve came up with Term Securities lending Facility (TSLF) that was aimed at providing the secured loans of Treasury securities to the primary dealers for 28-day terms (Bernanke, 1983; Doti and Larry, 1991; Ebersole, 1933).

According to Anari, James and Joseph (2005) fiscal policy was not used in the Great Depression in order to counter the declining economic activity for the first three years. However, the Governments had tried to counteract the stabilization effect brought by the reduced tax inflow. During this period, in United States and France, there was increasing deficit that could not be counteracted by the tax increases, and it amounted to 2.3 percent on average from 1933 to 1936. There were budgetary policy that were began at the start of the Great depression with an aim of combating the deficits at first but to no avail. This was basically true for United States and France. United States had small surpluses all over the twenties but there was no cyclical pattern. The government expenditure however continued to increase in early 1930s, and in 1932, there was a slight decrease in the tax revenues. This decline was then combated with massive tax increases across the board, mainly in lower and medium income groups. The earned tax credit was done away with, gift tax was provided, and the corporate income tax was increased slightly. Similarly, the general sale tax together with excise was also raised. Nevertheless, at the time, United Kingdom would still have budget surplus over the whole period from 1929 to 1936.

In the recent crisis, fiscal policy was significantly used in order to mitigate the downturn through allowing automatic stabilizers to work, provision of the stimulus packages, recapitalizing banks as well as providing guarantees for the banks together with firms. The level at which the downturn was combated due to the specific stimulus packaging is difficult to assess, however, the consensus is that it amounted to about one percent of the GDP, not only in 2009, but also in 2010 (Kehoe, Ruhl and Steinberg, 2012). Inherently, the stimulus levels in United States and China were higher, but in the EU they were lower. Notably, the automatic stabilizers did a significant job despite the fact that they were supported and not thwarted by the discretionary restrictive measure.

3.3.2 Protectionism and Structural Differences

As noted, Great depression was aggravated by the fact that every country tried to protect their own economy from the negative impacts of the world's depression. As a result, this made the average tariff rate to rise with 12.7 percent during the Great Depression. A specific form of protectionism widely used in the Smooth-Hawley Tariff Act of 1930, whereby, the United States tariffs on the imports were raised (Cargill and Thomas, 2006; Hetzel and Ralph, 2001; Huizinga and Luc, 2009). Similarly, duties in several other countries were raised as well. Despite the fact that it is difficult to find general indicators for protectionism, the customs inflow provides critical guidance on the protectionism. The Tariffs together with import duties were important during the Great Depression since they constituted a major source of revenue for the governments. In addition, through increasing the duties, the effect to protect the domestic producers was welcomed. The customs receipt in the relation to the GDP added up to about 0.6 percent for the United States between 1925 and 1928, however, it only changed slightly during the first years of the crisis, and then decreased in the following years. The Great depression resulted to a considerable reduction of trade, and this indicates the higher customs duties per unit of trade were high as well.

In the European countries, on the other hand, the level of custom inflows relative to the GDP was conspicuously higher from the beginning. The receipts basically increased in the build-up period. This was quite evident in France, Germany, and Austria. In United Kingdom, they were flat, but in Sweden, they decreased slightly since the beginning of 1929 to 1935. As a result, protectionism did not begin simultaneously with the Great Depression for United States, when measured by the custom receipts, however, it played a role in prolonging as well as deepening it. Moreover, it also seems to have been applied in the EU than in the United States.

The other indicator, which can be said to contain indirect information regarding protectionism, is the openness indicator. The Openness indicator combines the information on export along with the import shares in GDP. In 1929 to 1932 the openness indicator dropped from 34 percent to 20 percent. The fall was significantly less for the United States, but for Germany, United Kingdom, and France, it was nearly half.

3.4 Lessons from Global Financial Crises

One of crucial issues going forward is how to construct a resilient economic system. There have been numerous crises over the past 200 years despite the fact that the Great depression and GFC were of greater magnitude, and the worst. The emergences of the crises have been blamed on the bad behavior on the part of the financial system. However, the financial systems have always been behaving badly, and therefore, this is not a surprise. Similarly, the crisis does not indicate an end to the bad behavior. The global financial crisis has revealed massive lessons not only to the economists, but also to the common people as well. Some of the clear lessons from the crises include: there is need to strengthen the theoretical foundations upon which the regulatory bodies are built on, there is need to counter the widespread perverse incentives, there is need to relook at the underwriting matters, and also there is need to strengthen the regulations and supervisions of financial institutions

3.4.1 The Regulatory Bodies are Built on very Weak Theoretical Foundation

The major regulatory bodies, such as NFA are based on light regulations of the commercial bank, and even lighter regulation when it comes to the investment banks, and little for the shadow banking system regulation. The support for the lax regulation was reinforced through the central claim of the neoclassical financial economics that the capital market securities correctly in regard to the expected return and risk. The buyers and sellers of the financial securities were in a position to make optimal decisions that contributed to the risk being held by the ones who are able to manage it. The basic narrative that is related by the NFA indicates that relatively free financial market have a tendency of minimizing the possibility of financial crises along with government bailouts. Eggertsson (2008) argues that this theoretical cornerstone of the regulatory bodies is based on unrealistic assumption and hence it does not have any convincing empirical support. Consequently, the foundation of the regulatory bodies could be termed as weak.

3.4.2 Widespread Perverse Incentives

The financial system had been riddled with perverse incentives that induced key personnel in most of the financial institutions such as the commercial and investment banks and the private equity funds, mutual and pension funds and the insurance companies to assume excessive risks when the financial markets are buoyant. For instance, the growth of the mortgage securitization generated fee income to the mortgage and bank brokers who sold the loans, the banks and specialists institutions which serviced the securities, the investment bankers who packaged loans in securities, and the rating agencies which approved them. The top investment bank traders along with the executives received giant bonuses in which the risk taking generates high revenues. Another egregious examples of the perverse incentives includes the insurance giants AIG's Financial Production unit which gambled on the credit default swaps and this contributed to surprisingly high profits for the firm during the boom. These instances, shows that is rational for the top financial operatives to assume excessive risk in the bubble even when they are clearly aware of the fact that their decisions may cause a crash in the intermediate future. Bearing in mind that they do not have to return their bubble-year bonuses when the inevitable crisis comes along, and also they continue to receive the bonuses even during the crisis, they then come up with powerful incentives to pursue the high-risk and high-leveraging strategies. This further made the credit agencies to also be infected by the perverse incentives. According to Liu, Wang and Zha (2011) the global financial boom and the resulting crisis may not have occurred if the perverse incentives had not induced the credit rating agencies that will give absurdly high ratings to illiquid the non-transparent, structured financial products and collateralized loan obligations. Regulation of the financial markets will not be effective, therefore, unless there is substantial reduction of the perverse incentives that pervade the system.

3.4.3 Underwriting Matters

According to Huizinga and Luc (2009) underwriting is defined as the process of determining the credit worthiness of the borrowers through putting in place incentives that will help in ensuring payments are made as they come due. For the periods near the crisis, one of the evident issues is that the big institutions which are involved in lending, either reduced or eliminated underwriting.

Herkenhos, and Ohanian, (2012a) states that the efficient markets hypothesis that one does not require underwriting since the market is in a position to discover the proper prices for the securitized loans, and more importantly, lending is very easy and cheap there is no checking of the financial capacity of the borrower. Unfortunately, this often leads to Liar Loans along with NINJA loans that do not have job, income, or asset to bank on. Looking at the recent financial crises, there has been a deterioration of underwriting standards. The market discipline does not work since when some asset class is booming, the banks, in this case the lenders, expect that the prices of the assets is going to rise. The lenders will generally lend more relative to the value of asset or the expected cash flow. However, if things do not work out, the loans can then be refinanced or a collateral can be seized and sold. The lending market works like that until someone questions the boom, when it is discovered that the asset could have been overvalued and as a result this causes the prices to reverse course and collapsing making the borrowers run away and the lenders to be left insolvent.

In the Great Financial Crisis, the depositors in the money market mutual funds began to worry that their funds may not be in a position to guarantee that a dollar of their liability is worth a dollar, and therefore, causing a run. The shadow banks that depended on the rolling-over very short term liabilities found the rising discount applied to the collateral to a point that they could not refinance positions in assets. This contributed to a dramatic decline in the asset prices along with general liquidity crisis (Garriga,

Manuelli, and Peralta-Alva, 2012). In addition, it was also found out that the asset had been overvalued that even with Treasury extensions to guarantees together with trillion of dollars of lender last resort by the Federal bank, most people were not willing to refinance their loans. Consequently, since the financial institutions relied on each other, they discovered the dangers of interconnectedness. Consequently, if the financial institutions could embrace retrenched, tightening standards as well as cutting off loans to all but the most credit worthy, then they will avoid such a great mistake.

3.4.4 The Unregulated and Unsupervised Financial Institutions

The regulators allowed the financial to institutions to hold risky securities off their balance sheets in the SIVs even though there was no capital that was required to support them. The regulatory system, therefore, induced the crises by letting the institutions to move as much of their assets off-balance-sheet as possible.

Similarly, deregulation also allowed the financial conglomerates to become very large and complex to a point that the insiders along with the outsiders were not in a position to evaluate their risk. For instance, the Bank for the International Settlement let the national regulators to provide an opportunity for the banks to evaluate their own risk, and therefore, set their own capital requirements by having a statistical exercise that was based on the Value at Risk. In turn, the Government officials then ceded to banks the crucial aspects of regulatory power. According to Manuelli and Peralta-Alva (2011), this mode of assessment led to three fundamental flaws. One, there is no time in period that the historical data used to generate dependable estimate of the current risk. If the firms make use of the data from the past years, then during the boom periods, both for the Great Depression and Great Recession, VAR exercises would have indicated that the risk is minimal since the defaults and the capital losses on the securities are very low. Secondly, the models assume that the security prices are generated through a normal distribution, in which the likelihood of an observation will be beyond 95 percent, is infinitesimal. As a result, by allowing the financial institutions to estimate risk as well as set capital requirements on the assumption that the large losses may not happen made them to be vulnerable when the crises erupted. Thirdly, the asset price correlation matrix, which as a key determinant of the measured VAR assumes that the future price correlations will be similar to those of the recent past. Nevertheless, during the crises, the historical correlation matrix lost all the relation to the asset price dynamics and therefore, the actual risk was much higher than the risk estimates from the VAR exercises.

3.5 Conclusion

The study finds out thatGreat Recession resulted to a significant increase in unemployment, which affected workers disproportionately. The downturn was severe to a point that it had adverse effects on all the groups of workers and all regions across the world in terms of stagnant wages and substantial unemployment.

According to Reinhart and Kenneth (2009) the labor market deterioration from 2007 to 2009, after the Great Recession was accompanied by a historical cyclical negative relationship between job openings or vacancies and unemployment. Insecurity, uncertainty, and risk were pervasive within the labor market and have affected the older and younger workers alike. Various countries have initiated different response mechanisms that not only aimed at making these countries to stand again on their feet, but also to help them develop shock absorbers in case of such an occurrence. One of crucial issues going forward is how to construct a resilient economic system.

The two crises also put significant pressure to other structures such as education. The dramatic cyclical downturn of the Great Recession came in after a period of increase of wage inequality and educational wage differentials in Europe and United States.

Various response mechanisms were initiated in order to make countries to stand again on their feet, as well as help them develop shock absorbers in case of such an occurrence. One of the approaches that has been of keen interest is the Lisbon Strategy that is based on the need to increase productivity and competitiveness while enhancing social cohesion in the face of global competition and technology change. Similarly, the United States policy making during the Great Recession seems to be a reaction of the events of the 1930s, as well as efforts to avoid a severe meltdown as the one resulted from the Great depression. The study also reveals that in the recent crisis, fiscal policy was significantly used in order to mitigate the downturn through allowing automatic stabilizers to work, provision of the stimulus packages, recapitalizing banks as well as providing guarantees for the banks together with firms.

Other responses to the crises includes use of protectionism and structural differences, for instance the Smooth-Hawley Tariff Act of 1930, which is a specific form of protectionism widely used in whereby, the United States tariffs on the imports were raised, and raising of duties as evidenced in several other countries as well.

The crises revealed that the major regulatory bodies, such as NFA, are based on light regulations of the commercial bank, and even lighter regulation when it comes to the investment banks, and little for the shadow banking system regulation. Moreover, it was also clear that the financial system had been riddled with perverse incentives that induced key personnel in most of the financial institutions such as the commercial and investment banks and the private equity funds, mutual and pension funds and the insurance companies to assume excessive risks when the financial markets are buoyant. Also, the regulatory system, therefore, induced the crises by letting the institutions to move as much of their assets off-balance-sheet as possible.

Chapter 4
COPING WITH ANOTHER GLOBAL FINANCIAL CRISIS: IS THERE NEED FOR NEW BODIES

4.1 Introduction

The two economic crisis questions the sustainability of our financial, social and ecological systems. This also raises the question of how prepared we are to a third economic crisis. Financial crises have happened in the past, and will also happen in the time to come, however, an economic crisis as profound as the Great Recession and Great Depression can be avoided. It is therefore, quite clear that there is need to have greater supervision and regulations that should foster countries to develop structures that will help in overcoming such a crisis.

In this chapter, therefore, the existing structures will be analyzed in order to find out the gaps that exist, as well as whether their capability are in question. This will not only cover the economic structures but also the ecological and social structures as well. The chapter will also seek to identify whether there is need to have new institutions in place that would guide recovery process in case of another economic crisis.

4.2 Economic Perspective

Hodson and Quaglia (2009) argue that the two financial crises are not as a result of free markets failure. Instead, they are classic examples of the undesirable unintended consequences of government intervention, not only through expansionary monetary policy, but also through misguided attempts to bolster the prevailing market conditions. Similarly, Carmassi, Grosand Micossi (2009)points out that there has been several financial crises that have occurred in the past, and yet, there are others that are likely to occur in the future, but significant economic crisis as then one resulting from Great Depression and Great Recession can be avoided. For instance, if after the each of the Great Recession broke, the government in the wealthy countries did not suddenly wake up and adopted the Keynesian policies of reducing the interest rates that increased the liquidity drastically as well as engaged in fiscal expansion, the crises would have probably done more damage to the economy more than what the Great Depression did. Inherently, capitalism is unstable and the crises are intrinsic to it, however, provided that a lot has been done in order to avoid the repetition of Great Depression crisis, is not sufficient to rely on the cyclical character of the financial crises or even on the greedy character of the financists in order to explain such a serious crisis. According to Cohen (2008), the struggle for easy and large capital gains in financial transactions as well as for the corresponding bonuses for individual traders is stronger as compared to the struggle for profits in the production and services as well. Most of the economists work with a special kind of commodity that has a fictitious asset that relies on the convention together with the confidence, which includes, financial assets and money or financial contractors, while on the other hand, the entrepreneurs deal with real commodities, real products and real services. Even though the economists call their assets products and the new types of financial contracts innovations, it does not change their nature. Money can be created but it can also disappear with relative facility, which makes finance and speculations to be twin brothers then. In speculation, the financial agents are normally permanent subject to the self-fulfilling prophecies as well as to the phenomenon that representatives of the Regulation School call self-referential rationality, while Hodson and Quaglia (2009)refers to it as reflectivity. Basically, they buy assets predicting that their price will eventually rise and the prices will actually go up because their purchases pushes the prices up. Then as the financial operations became more complex, the intermediary agents often emerge between the individual investors and the banks or the exchanges, which includes traders who do not get similar incentives as their principles but they are motivated by short-term gains that are made to increase their bonuses, stocks or bonds.

It is also worth noting that finance can also get distorted or dangerous when it is not oriented to the financing production and commerce, rather to financing treasury operations. This is a nicer euphemism for speculation, and on the part of business firms and commercial banks along with other financial institutions, the speculation without credit has limited scope. Specifically, they have financed and leveraged scope which makes it risky and boundless since when the indebtedness of the financial investors together with the leverage of the financial institutions become too great, the investors and the banks then come to the knowledge that risk has become insupportable, and the herd effect will then prevail, as it did in October 2008. This led to loss of confidence that crept in in the preceding months and then turned into panic, following this, the crisis broke.

Since the Great Depression, there has been a significant social learning. In 1930s Keynes together with Kalecki came up with a new economic theory that sought to explain how the economic system works along with rendering the economic policy making much more effective in stabilizing the economic cycles, however, sensible people were in a position to alert the politicians and economists to the dangers of unfettered markets. In 1954, John Galbraith published a classical book on the Great Depression, and also Charles Kindleberger published another in 1973. Since then, there has several other books that has been published which have provided learning that has been helpful to the governments in building institutions, specifically central banks, as well as developing competent regulatory systems, not only at the national level, but also at the international level so that they can be in a position to control credit and at the same time to avoid or reduce the intensity along with the scope of financial crises. However, since 70s, a fundamental Keynesian theory that linked finance, uncertainty and crisis was developed by Hyman Minsky. Basically, the theory discusses economic stagnation and also identifies financial fragility as the main cause of crisis (Cohen, 2008). That is, the increasing instability in the financial system is as a result of a process of increasing the autonomy of the financial instruments and of credit from the real side of economy. Minsky also claims that the economic crises and the financial crises are endogenous to the capitalist system. As such, the essential difference between the classical and neo classical, and the Keynesian economics is the importance of uncertainty. Since there is existence of uncertainty, the economic units are not in a position to maintain the equilibrium between their cash payment commitments and the normal sources of cash owing to the reason that the two variables only operate in the future, and the future is also uncertain. For this reason, the intrinsically irrational fact of uncertainty is therefore needed. Moreover, as the economic units tend to be optimist in the long-term, the booms will tend to be euphoric while the financial vulnerability of the economic system will then tend to increase. As such, this brings us to Dyson (2002) point of view that when the tolerance of the financial system to the shocks has been decreased through three phenomena that accumulate over a prolonged boom, then the triggering device in the financial instability could be the financial distress of a unit. The three phenomena includes the growth of financial (the balance sheet and portfolio) payments that are relative to the income payments, the decrease in the relative weight of the outside as well as guaranteed assets in the totality of the financial assets values, and thirdly the building into the financial structure of the asset prices that depicts the boom or the euphoric expectations.

Carmassi, Grosand Micossi (2009) argues that if the economists together with the financial regulators relied on the necessary theory along with the necessary organizational institutions as described above, they would have a chance of avoiding a major crisis as the one exhibited during the Great Recession. However, it was not possible to avoid it even after ensuring impressive economic principles after the Great Depression. Things changed after what Deeg and O'Sullivan (2009) refers to 30 glorious years when President Nixon decided to suspend the convertibility of the United States dollar in 1971. This resulted to disappearance of the relationship between money and real assets, and money would depend on confidence or trust. Although trust is the cement of every society, confidence loses a foundation or standard and may become ephemeral or fragile. This started happening in 1971. For this reason, Cohen (2008) claimed that the development of the modern banking system is the crucial reason why the market economies of the former two centuries has been successful, but the privatization of the foreign exchange risk in the 1970s increased the market risk significantly. The fixed exchange rate that was a foundation for economic stability then disappeared in 1971.

More importantly, there is no doubt about the immediate causes of the recent crisis. Deeg and O'Sullivan (2009) summarize the causes to two main ones: the outcome of the deliberate deregulation of the financial markets, and the outcome of the decision not to regulate the financial innovations together with the treasury banking practices. As a result, the global crisis is mainly as a result of the floating of the dollar in the 1970s, together with the euphemistically named regulatory reform that was preached and enacted in the 1980s by the neoliberal ideologues.

This realization is easy to comprehend on looking at the competent financial regulation together with the commitment to the social values and social rights that emerged following the 1930s depression. The regulation and the commitment to the social values and social rights were in a position to produce the 30 glorious years of capitalism between 1940s and 1970s. However, after the deregulation of the financial markets in the 1980s, and the Keynesian theories were forgotten, the neoclassical economics and public choice theories became mainstream, and the neoliberal ideas became hegemonic, the financial instability came knocking but it was well realized in during the recent financial crisis. As a result, it would be prudent to claim that deregulation along with the attempts to do away with the welfare state transformed the thirty years that followed to "black years of neoliberaisation" (Dyson, 2002).

The Neoliberalism together with the finacialization in the context of financial and commercial globalization. However, although commercial globalization was useful in the development of capitalism, in that, it helped in the diminution of the time together with the cost of transport along with the communications support of both the international trade and the international production, the financial globalization along with the financialization were not natural per say. In actual sense, both financial globalization and financialization can be said to be two perversions of the capitalist development. Cohen(2008)perceived this idea and claimed that the financial sphere describes the advanced spearhead of capital, where operations normally achieve the highest degree of mobility, as well as where the gap between the operators priorities and the world will need to be more acute. Consequently, globalization may have been limited to commerce, and this will take into consideration the trade liberalization and not the financial liberalization, which led the developing countries, with an exception of the fast growing Asian countries, to lose the control they had on the exchange rates and also to become victims of the recurrent balance of payment crises. Carmassi, Grosand Micossi (2009) claims that if the financial opening had been limited to the capitalist system, then it would not only been much efficient, but also it would have been more stable. Actually, it is not by chance that the fast growing Asian countries were in a position to engage actively in the commercial globalization, but they actually limited the financial liberalization.

Despite the fact that globalization was a consequence of technological change, that was inevitable, it does not indicate that the capitalist system is not a natural form of the economic and social system in that it can be systematically be changed by people as expressed in the institutions and culture. However, the institutions are not conditioned only by the level of economic together with the technological development as neoliberal economic determinist would assert. The institutions also do not exist in a vacuum as well as they are not determined, but they are dependent on the values along with the political will. These institutions are not only socially embedded, but her are culturally embedded as well, and they are also defined or regulated by state system that is not just a superstructure, but an integral part of the economic and social system. Actually, the institutions describe each society's division between the powerless and the powerful, where the former are normally associated to the winning group of capitalist rentiers and finacist, who may include the financial executives and traders along with consultants who gained power as capitalism become finance-led.

4.3 Policy

Carmassi, Grosand Micossi (2009) argues that the Austrian theory shows that the boom,that normally results to the financial crises, begins when the central banks create excessive amount of money along with when the banks find that they are not in a position to lend more without acquiring new savings from the public. With the new funds then, the banks will tend to lower their interest rates in order to attract new borrower. The lower interest rate may bring a notion that the public is saving more and therefore, it is more patient, this will then justify the longer term projects that firms will find profitable at the lower interest rates provided by the banks. When the lower interest rates are as a result of actual savings, then this notion will be true. However, when the lower interest rates are forced, or are as a result of an expansionary monetary policy, then they will be disconnected from the public's real willingness to wait.

Inherently, as producers come for more money from the banks in order to invest in long-tem projects under the illusion that the members of public are willing to wait, then capital goods will be created, purchased or refitted in order to engage in the longer processes. Labor is transferred from the production of consumption goods so as to work on the new projects. The prices and wages also rise up, even when the projects are not sustainable, and the results is the observed measures of boom such as unemployment falling, the profits and GDP rising. Nevertheless, the boom cannot last for long owing to the reason that the growth is not financed by the public real willingness to save, but through an illusion that was created by the monetary expansion. The inflation also causes the interest rates to be low artificially, and this sends a false signal regarding the public's preferences.

Following this, the entrepreneurs will start competing to purchase the capital and the labor that they require for projects and this will basically lead to rising of prices of the inputs so high to a point that the producers realize the projects may not be in a position to be completed profitably. For this reason, the producers may then abandon the projects and this will result to sudden fall of the prices of capital and financial assets as well as wages. Moreover, the unemployment rates will increase in the sectors that are associated with the capital goods industries. This will then welcome the bust phase of the cycle, as the stock prices will fall, and the asset prices will deflate, and in the end, the overall economic activity slows and unemployment rates rises further. According to Hodson and Quaglia (2009), the capital goods that are associated with longer production processes will then be instantaneously and costlessly be converted to new uses in the consumption goods sectors. The labor will also follow the same trend such that the workers who lost jobs working, for instance in research and development, will not be in a position to immediately find a job in another sector.

According to the Austrian theory, the boom results from making economic mistakes, and it is during the bust that the mistakes can be corrected. For instance, the false interest rate signal generated through expansionary monetary policy will lead to mistakes that should be eventually revealed. After the unsustainability of the boom has become clear, then it is the bust that corrects the mistakes. The unemployed capital together with the labor shows that the entrepreneurs are learning from their misallocation and the attempts by both the owners of capital and workers to make new ways of creating value. Similarly, the recession then manifests itself as the purging and the correction of errors that were induced by the artificial boom.

Going back to the various measures of the money supply along with the related interest rates, it is clear that the United States Federal Reserve System expansionary policy was behind driving of the interest rates down. Inherently, the Greenspan era Federal Reserve Bank adopted expansionary policy as a part of its attempt to pull the United States economy out of the small post 9/11 recession (Cohen, 2008). As a result, the Federal Reserve Bank came up with new reserves in order to make the Federal Funds to fall to the 1 percent range for that particular period. It actually stayed well below the recent historic norms for a long period of time before 2007. For approximately two years of the said period, the real Federal Funds rate, which is given by subtracting the rate of inflation from the nominal rate, was actually below zero, and this implied that people were paid to borrow.

In accordance to the Austrian perspective, the expansionary policy refers to that which pushes the market rates to less than a rate consistent with the public's time preferences that is known as the natural rate of interest. The challenge of expansionary policy is that it is normally very hard to know the ease of monetary policy since the natural rate of interest is not directly observable. Dyson (2002) provides a crude estimate of the natural rate together with a technique that suggests that the monetary policy was excessively easy after the dot.com collapse and that it was to an extent that could not be compared with any since the inflationary 1970s. Inherently, this proves that the estimated natural together with the real Federal Funds rate began diverging in 2001, and by 2005, the actual real Federal Funds rate was five percentage points lower than the expected natural real Federal Funds rate. Carmassi, Grosand Micossi (2009), however, claims that whatever, the imperfection of the previous estimate of the natural rate are, a five percentage point difference may not be explained through such imperfections alone and will most likely reflect a degree of expansionary policy. According to Deeg and O'Sullivan (2009) the seasonally adjusted growth in M2, which is the widely accepted monetary aggregate in the United States, was approximately 32.5 percent between 2002 and 2006. As a result, the money supply expanding, along with the interest rates being below the natural levels, then the evidence of the Australian boom theory is strong.

This then brings us to the question "can policy protect us from future financial crisis?" Looking at the former financial crises with regard to the Austrian theory, then it is possible that given the role that was played by the government in causing the boom together with the bust, then there will be skepticism that the government of course can do much in order to cure the problem. According to Cohen (2008), the structural incentives of the political process indicate that even if there are a number of things that the government ought to do in order to help the situation, then it is not prudent to ignore the question whether political actors should have the incentives to do the things and the only things that should concede their role in safeguarding the world against any future crisis.

Inherently, it is worth noting that even though the boom and the bust cycle looks like a microeconomic failure, there are a whole series of failures of microeconomic level. That is, the problem is not that the macroeconomic aggregates such as the GDP or unemployment that needs to be corrected. The problem is actually a manifestation of misallocation of resourcesin the various markets and therefore this leads to the distortion of the interest rates together with other prices that are associated with the boom. Correcting this will therefore require knowledgeable policy makers who will be in a position to figure out where resources should be given real costs and the preferences. In solving problems of this manner that the markets and the entrepreneurs who operate in them are good at, then it is good to set markets free to engage in the discovery process.

According to Eastwood, Holmes and Quaglia (2009) the history of several stimulus together with recovery programmes shows that governments will not limit themselves into policies that mainstream the economic theory only. However, when given the intellectual rationale to intervene, the politicians will make that an excuse in order to propose as well as pass a number of items irrespective of whether they fit the economist model of pump-priming stimulus. For instance, Carmassi, Grosand Micossi (2009) reports that the debate over the Obama Administration's stimulus package in the United States demonstrates this sort of concern as did the debate over his proposed budget in 2009. In the two cases, there were claims that were made that the expenditures were necessary for economic recovery, and yet the significant resources pledged to education, healthcare and the environment which have no known relationship to the economic models of recovery. Similarly, Roosevelt Administration had also set a similar precedent during the Great Depression even after Keynes was moved to note that many of the proposals from the Administration seemed more like reform than recovery. Such ways will tend to create additional costs that might offset any imagined gains and can also slow the recovery of the private sector through adopting policies that may pose threats to the security of property and even the possibility of the earned profits.

Hague and Harrop (2010) reveals that the downturn in the economic activity that we associate with the recession or bust is, with respect to the Austrian view, the economy in the process of shedding capital along with labor from where it is no longer profitable. This is in accordance to the fallible nature of people and their imperfectness that despite being superior, the discovery process of the market shows that moving the resources to where they will be productive will consume time.

Dyson (2002) states that even if the practical political problems may be addressed, the more fundamental point is that the theory should always drive people to be skeptical of the government-driven solutions. That is most macroeconomic policy recommendations are focused on the aggregates such as investment, unemployment and consumption. This focus then obscures the necessary adjustment processes as revealed through the Austrian theory, which has to do with reallocation of resources in the sectors in the microeconomic level. Looking at the policies that will create jobs or even expand the government spending in order to compensate for supposedly insufficient private sector activity is not a prudent choice. In recalling the core of the Austrian theory with respect to how inflation tends to drive the interest rates artificially and as a result causing the misallocation of labor and capital among several sectors, with capital being malinvested in the earlier stages of production processes. The theory normally termed as overinvestment theory, which according to Carmassi, Grosand Micossi (2009), is wrong perspective of the theory. Actually, there are some overinvestments, but for a short period of time, however, the real problem is that the resources are being utilized in the wrong places. The traditional aggregates could not be in a position to show any change in the total level of investment even after the resources are misallocated between the earlier stages of production such as research and development, and then to other sectors. The entrepreneurs at the former stages of production will idle their capital and labor because the profitability is shrinking and their counterparts in the later stages will also consider whether to purchase new capital or hire new labor. Moreover, the prices of the capital goods along with the wages of labor might also have to go down significantly in order to make such moves profitable as well as the capital may also require refitting and labor retraining in order to make a better fit for the bust economy. This adjustment will obviously need skilful judgment of the entrepreneurs as they are guided by the market prices while the profit and loss signal so as to determine where capital and labor idle can be redeployed profitably. Similarly, it is not an issue of there being too much labor of too much capital, rather it is about whether specific capital goods or labor are appropriate for a specific stage of production in a specific production process. It is about recognizing that capital cannot be regarded as undifferentiated aggregate, instead as the heterogeneous capital goods, which show that it cannot be instantly, be reallocated, and without cost, from the early stages to the later stages in accordance to what the mainstream theory tends to imply. Similarly, labor also will follow the same principle as well. In trying to substitute the government spending for the private investments, then it will suffer same problem since it overlooks both the shifts in the labor and capital that is required by the recovery together with the comparative inefficiency of the government and the private expenditures. Inherently, through boosting the aggregate measures of consumption along with the investment by a form of government expenditure, the existing resources may not get reallocated away from the sectors that may artificially be stimulated by the boom to the sectors where the consumers may wish to spend. Comprehending this point as well as understanding why the government stimulus programmesmay not work will need a vision of capital as well as that of production that are less on the statistical aggregates but more on the microeconomic coordination processes.

Deeg and O'Sullivan (2009) supports this argument and states that only the aggregates that are located in the context of the market that have the knowledge along with the feedback processes to make the decisions that will help in reallocation of resources quickly and effectively as possible. More importantly, even in taking out the inevitable politicization of the process, the government stimulus programmes may be less effective at pointing out where the resources have been misallocated as well as where there is need to go. Moreover, if the boom comes in the time that the mistakes are made, and the bust is the way through which the market corrects the mistakes, the government interference with subtle as well as complex correction processes will only delay it. Only the decentralized decision-making as well as learning processes of the market will help in accomplishing the millions of corrections that may take place in myriad of microeconomic markets.

Is there any positive programme that would help in safeguarding countries against a major crisis? It is important to first note that governments will have to do something. Actually, saying that government should not participate, then it is synonymous to saying that people should also do nothing. However, in actual sense, safeguarding will depend on the active and creative entrepreneurship on the part of economic actors. Involving all the stakeholders is likely to achieve something, and actually, according to Cohen (2008), for the entrepreneur-driven process to happen effectively, then the policy makers should not interfere with the process by attempting to create a stable and predictable environment that the entrepreneurs should operate. The policy makers should try to minimize the Higgsian regime uncertainty in order to facilitate the countless individual adjustments that will constitute the recovery. Secondly, they should also be involved in the radical supply side deregulation in the product and labor market in order to enhance the movement of factors of production to different users.

According to the Austrian theory, the root problem of the financial crisis is not poor polices alone, but also institutions. Consequently, coming up with a precautionary measure with regard to future financial crisis, the there is need to address the underlying institutional causes of the crisis, such as the ability of the central banks expanding credit at their discretion and as a result initiating the boom and subsequent bust.

Carmassi, Grosand Micossi (2009)suggest that ending the privileges that are associated with central banks as well as allowing privately owned bank to also issue currency competitively and enabling them to come up with inter-bank institutions like private clearing houses similar to the ones in the 19th century. Having clearing houses may provide a chance to the financial institutions of taking on many of the tasks of the central banks in a more efficient manner as it was before the clearing houses were rendered unnecessary by the conception of the central banks. Having a free banking system is likely to stop the credit expansions that normally generates the boom and the bust cycle, which are accompanied by recessions. Bringing the central banking system to an end, will also make it harder to the governments to borrow into significant debts since it will remove the chance of using the central bank in buying up the debt that the public does not want. As the stimulus plans were adopted by a number of Western countries together with the ongoing unsustainable welfare state commitments, keep on driving the burden of the government debt across the world up, the temptation of using inflation to buy the debt also continues to grow. If the governments succumb to such temptation, then there is likelihood of setting in motion another chain of events that may create yet another, and may be a worse, boom and bust cycle. It is therefore, important to separate the money production from the state and government, and this will be a very important institutional change that will not only help in recovery but also in preventing the future, and probably worse recessions.

4.4 Is There need for New Institutions?

Both the Great recession and the Great Depression questions the sustainability of the current financial system, more so on the relationship between the nations and the debtors without risking a system-wide failure. As it is evident in the previous discussion, there is need to have greater supervision, transparency and regulation. Although, there has been institutions that have been set towards achieving these issues, the debate over whether to have new independent institutions still continues.

The harmonization of the national banking regulations has been well achieved through deregulations. Deregulations began in 1950s after the financial institutions were granted freedom of establishment across state lines. Further, another directive that laid out the responsibility for the nation states to supervise the transnational banks that have obligations in other countries. Deregulation was then followed by the financial innovation together with financial concentration at different parts of the world, that is, different countries. This provided a perfect avenue for new banks that tend to accept too many risks through innovative solutions so as to break into the market (Hodson and Quaglia, 2009). Consequently, this indicates more bubbles and significant economic growth. By 1990s, there were several banking directives that comprised of transparency-enforcing directives like the Bank Accounts Directive, the prudential behavior Directives like the Own Funds Directive, and the Second Banking Directive. The Basel committee on Banking Supervision also set up several rules, for instance, BASEL I which sets out the minimum requirements for the internationally active banks, and the BASEL II that allowed the banks to add risky assets on top of that. The BASEL is however, associated with the current indiscipline and absence of transparency. The present rules were short in limiting banks and allowed them to go beyond their means. The cross-border risks are mainly taken by the banks together with their mergers that undertake wide range of financial activities. As a result, the need for new restrictions is now evident. Nevertheless, there is a serious issue concerning the credibility with the restrictions when considering that the actors who normally develop the rules are the bankers themselves together with people who have best knowledge of what needs to be liberalized for their activities (Dyson, 2002). Moreover, private organizations such as the International Accounting Standards Board (IASB) and the International Financial Reporting Standards (IFRS) are funded as well as dominated by the industries from United States and United Kingdom. The publicly listed companies has been obliged to use the standards set by these organizations, and therefore, this is to say that the business rules are created by the private regulatory entities.

4.4.1 Capabilities of the Current Regulatory Bodies

While the Federal Reserve Bank is responsible for the United States economic and monetary policy, the ECB has similar mandate in EU (European Central Bank, 2009). During the financial crises, it was not a problem with the institutional coordination and crisis management, rather it was regulatory system from crisis prevention. The Crisis prevention encompasses the financial supervision that is mainly carried out at the national level, and the financial regulation. As a result, the capacity of these major regulatory bodies to regulate with the major banks has been under question (McCormick, 2007).

Carmassi, Grosand Micossi (2009) points out that the financial structure has two main inseparable aspects. It is composed of not just the structures of the political economy through which credit is created, but also the monetary systems, which determine the relative values of the different moneys in which the credit is dominated. This therefore, raises a question whether the regulator bodies are underdeveloped or whether there is need to have additional bodies. An efficient financial market will require distribution of power among the actors with specific tasks. For this reason, Hodson and Quaglia (2009) acknowledges that the current regulatory bodies failed to operate the financial regulatory body. Moreover, they did not manage to coordinate reliable supervision of the financial entities (Mayes, 2009). Consequently, Held and McGrew (2007) suggests that having more institutions will lead to greater rivalry, but also will enhance financial stability.

4.4.2 Can Rules be set without New Institutions?

Cohen (2008) argues that monetary system is a symbiosis of both the market and political authority, and that the state intervention does not have to be negative in limiting free marketing. This can be done through setting rules that the financial market and trade operate. For instance, in order to avoid the massive bubbles that are caused by the innovations, a financial authority may help in regulating how money may be used. Bearing in mind that the economic growth, investor's confidence together with the competitiveness relies on the banks, shareholders and the direction of regulation, there is need for the government to develop rules that favor financial entities and corporations to look attractive through appropriate business climate. Actually, the government needs to seek to prove their credibility together with the consistency of their policies in accordance to the degree to which they inspire the confidence of the investors. In accordance to this, the constitutional and political initiatives in the sphere of money should be linked to the imposition of the micro-economic and macro-economic discipline in such a way that they intend to underpin the power of capital and civil society. Harvey (2006) states that it is however, unlikely for the governments to suddenly be willing to restrict the global investors from putting their investments at risk. This is actually a significant argument in the favor of creating a supranational authority that will aid in setting rules and conduct supervision. Nevertheless, institutions have always been in the states' sphere of influence.

4.5 Conclusion

This chapter seeks to understand how prepared we are to a third economic crisis. Financial crises have happened in the past, and will also happen in the time to come, however, can we avoid an economic crisis as profound as the Great Recession and Great Depression?

The study reveals that the two financial crises are not as a result of free markets failure. Instead, they are classic examples of the undesirable unintended consequences of government intervention, not only through expansionary monetary policy, but also through misguided attempts to bolster the prevailing market conditions. Evidence from the Great Recession shows that adoption of the Keynesian policies of reducing the interest rates that increases the liquidity drastically as well as engaging in fiscal expansion, another future crisis may be managed and the damage that can result from it may be reduced. The study also notes that having clearing houses may provide a chance to the financial institutions of taking on many of the tasks of the central banks in a more efficient manner as it was before the clearing houses were rendered unnecessary by the conception of the central banks. Having a free banking system is likely to stop the credit expansions that normally generates the boom and the bust cycle, which are accompanied by recessions, as noted by the Austrian theory. Bringing the central banking system to an end will also make it harder to the governments to borrow into significant debts since it will remove the chance of using the central bank in buying up the debt that the public does not want. As the stimulus plans were adopted by a number of Western countries together with the ongoing unsustainable welfare state commitments, keep on driving the burden of the government debt across the world up, the temptation of using inflation to buy the debt also continues to grow. If the governments succumb to such temptation, then there is likelihood of setting in motion another chain of events that may create yet another, and may be a worse, boom and bust cycle. It is therefore, important to separate the money production from the state and government, and this will be a very important institutional change that will not only help in recovery but also in preventing the future, and probably worse recessions.

The failure of the current regulatory bodies is also quite evident as seen in through the study. The Crisis prevention encompasses the financial supervision that is mainly carried out at the national level, and the financial regulation. As a result, the capacity of these major regulatory bodies to regulate with the major banks has been under question. Hodson and Quaglia (2009) acknowledges that the current regulatory bodies failed to operate the financial regulatory body. Moreover, they did not manage to coordinate reliable supervision of the financial entities. Consequently, Held and McGrew (2007) suggests that having more institutions will lead to greater rivalry, but also will enhance financial stability. It is therefore, quite clear that there is need to have greater supervision and regulations that should foster countries to develop structures that will help in overcoming such a crisis.

Chapter 5
CONCLUSION

5.1 Introduction

The intent of this dissertation is to analyze the effects of the two major economic crises, the Great Depression and the Global Financial Crisis of 2008, with a focus on the social and ecological aspects. Hans Sennholz (1969) in his article on the Great Depression closed by asking a question, "Can it (Great Depression) happen again? The question though not answered has been answered by the circumstances and time. In the wake of 2008, the stock market experienced another crash that affected the world economy in almost a similar way that the Great depression. Notably, the dissertation finds that answer to the question lies on whether the government and regulators are willing and what they will do in response to the lessons acquired from the two major financial crises, the Great Depression of 1930, and the Great Recession of 2008. In this chapter, we look at the summary of the analysis in the previous chapters, in order to guide the recommendations offered in the way forward section.

5.2 Summary

The study finds that the 'Great Depression' came after the 1929 stock market crash and marked the biggest economic crisis that the world had experienced at the time. The depth together with the length of the crisis and the subsequent suffering caused has been legendary. As a result, when the Global Financial Crisis hit in 2007, most believed that the world is about to experience another depression of equal scale and termed it as the Great Recession.

A significant gap on the impacts of the Great Depression and Global Financial crises of 2008 exists since, the examination of these impacts have been biased on the financial aspect, and therefore, it is also important to look at the social and ecological aspects of the two economic crisis as well. This dissertation therefore, contributes to a broader understanding of the nature of the financial crises. Similarly, it also serves as an exemplary case since the financial crisis may have become a revolutionary event for challenging the deregulated free-market through reinforcing the need for regulation and possible institutions in the global level.

Chapter two looks at the pre-crises environment through establishing the stimulating resemblances of the Great Depression and the Great Recession. When the two great financial crisis are examined then it comes out clear that there are significant amount of similarities between the Great Depression and the Great Recession. The similarities of the Great Depression and the Great Recession tend to also indicate that their causes are also similar to each other. The two financial crises are characterized by a boom that results from making economic mistakes, and it is during the bust that the mistakes can be corrected. Specifically, the false interest rate signal generated through expansionary monetary policy will lead to mistakes that should be eventually revealed. After the unsustainability of the boom has become clear, then it is the bust that corrects the mistakes. Great depression was strongly sawn by intellectuals or institutional scholars who always advocated for enactment of protective and wage laws. The congressman and women give comments that reflect their experiences and backgrounds while in college, and therefore much blame for the both depression and recession is closely related to the teaching availed in colleges and universities by scholars, for instance, during the 1929 period, everyone was hoping for the better in economy and little consequences were expected to come out of inflation except the Austrians who expected that there could be challenges and breakdowns in stock markets.

Chapter three looks at the post crises environment with a view of establishing whether the crises have been effectively managed. The study finds out that Great Recession resulted to a significant increase in unemployment, which affected workers disproportionately. The downturn was severe to a point that it had adverse effects on all the groups of workers and all regions across the world in terms of stagnant wages and substantial unemployment. The two crises also put significant pressure to other structures such as education. The dramatic cyclical downturn of the Great Recession came in after a period of increase of wage inequality and educational wage differentials in Europe and United States. Various response mechanisms were initiated in order to make countries to stand again on their feet, as well as help them develop shock absorbers in case of such an occurrence. Other responses to the crises includes use of protectionism and structural differences, for instance the Smooth-Hawley Tariff Act of 1930, which is a specific form of protectionism widely used in whereby, the United States tariffs on the imports were raised, and raising of duties as evidenced in several other countries as well. The crises revealed that the major regulatory bodies, such as NFA, are based on light regulations of the commercial bank, and even lighter regulation when it comes to the investment banks, and little for the shadow banking system regulation. Moreover, it was also clear that the financial system had been riddled with perverse incentives that induced key personnel in most of the financial institutions such as the commercial and investment banks and the private equity funds, mutual and pension funds and the insurance companies to assume excessive risks when the financial markets are buoyant. Also, the regulatory system, therefore, induced the crises by letting the institutions to move as much of their assets off-balance-sheet as possible.

In chapter four, thechapter seeks to understand how prepared we are to a third economic crisis, and also tries to answer the question whether we can avoid an economic crisis as profound as the Great Recession and Great Depression. The chapter reveals that the two financial crises are not as a result of free markets failure. Instead, they are classic examples of the undesirable unintended consequences of government intervention, not only through expansionary monetary policy, but also through misguided attempts to bolster the prevailing market conditions. Further, having a free banking system is likely to stop the credit expansions that normally generates the boom and the bust cycle, which are accompanied by recessions, as noted by the Austrian theory.

The failure of the current regulatory bodies is also quite evident as seen in through the study. The Crisis prevention encompasses the financial supervision that is mainly carried out at the national level, and the financial regulation. As a result, the capacity of these major regulatory bodies to regulate with the major banks has been under question. Hodson and Quaglia

(2009) acknowledge that the current regulatory bodies failed to operate the financial regulatory body. Moreover, they did not manage to coordinate reliable supervision of the financial entities. Consequently, Held and McGrew (2007) suggests that having more institutions will lead to greater rivalry, but also will enhance financial stability. The global financial crises have in the last century been one of the main assaults of the global economic stability to have occurred. It basically describes the regulatory failure in the modern history. It is therefore, quite clear that there is need to have greater supervision and regulations that should foster countries to develop structures that will help in overcoming such a crisis.

5.3 Way Forward

Clearly, neoliberal financial policy has failed to curb the financial crises, and instead, ithas promoted boundless desire for profit. Moreover, it also creates a totally different reality to the self-market demand. In this study, the inherent failure of a deregulated market have been exposed that is accompanied by financial innovations which do not help in ensuring sustainability or the wellbeing of societies, more so in the long run. This neoliberalism has also contributed towards existence of unequal distribution of resources in which the concentration of welfare and power has dramatically increased. There is no doubt, then, that there is need to have more coordination in regulatory policies at a global level (Herkenhoand Ohanian, 2012). This realization is easy to comprehend on looking at the competent financial regulation together with the commitment to the social values and social rights that emerged following the 1930s depression. The regulation and the commitment to the social values and social rights were in a position to produce the 30 glorious years of capitalism between 1940s and 1970s. However, after the deregulation of the financial markets in the 1980s, and the Keynesian theories were forgotten, the neoclassical economics and public choice theories became mainstream, and the neoliberal ideas became hegemonic, the financial instability came knocking but it was well realized in during the recent financial crisis.

As Kehoe, Ruhl and Steinberg (2012) puts it, Great Recession and Great Depression are classic examples of the unwelcome unintended consequences of government intervention, through the use of expansionary monetary policy. Moreover, the misguided interventions were also aimed at bolstering the housing market in the United States in the wake of the Great Recession. The study finds that this combination resulted to unsustainable boom, with the focus of the boom being a policy-induced bubble within the housing sector together with the resulting collection of the financial instruments that were built on the bubble. As a result of the occurrence of the boom, that is, the misallocation of the resources coming from false interest rate signals, it is then crucial to characterize the boom as the making of mistakes while the inevitable bust as the correction of these mistakes. As a result, one of the ways that will help in correcting the misallocation is to let the entrepreneurs to figure out where the resources will need to go as being guided by the market prices, profits and losses. The government spending programs are also evidently too blunt as well as too politicized as instruments that can do that job. Depending on such instruments then, it would create further mistakes. In the long run, then, the damage of the boom as well as the bust cycle can be avoided by cutting off at the root through formulating reforms regarding the monetary system that will end the privileges that is accorded to the central banks. More importantly, getting the government out of banking systems may also be the best way that will help the banks out of the government as well as to end the disastrous boom together with the bust cycles that have been characterized in the last century.

It is also quite important to resolve the failed institutions. The failure of the current regulatory bodies is also quite evident as seen in through the study. The Crisis prevention encompasses the financial supervision that is mainly carried out at the national level, and the financial regulation. As a result, the capacity of these major regulatory bodies to regulate with the major banks has been under question. In resolving the failed institutions, there need to put in mind three crucial factors. One, the regulators should be in a position to address the asymmetric information problems that result to the financial panics. Keane and Rogerson (2012) suggest that the bad banks can be quarantined in order to alleviate the asymmetric information. This worked earlier during the great depression when some form of certification or quarantine of the toxic assets that result to asymmetric information concerns was done, although it changed later in 1970sAfter being able to stabilize the system, the regulators should then resolve the insolvent institutions. The resolution process should articulate the means through which the trustees can return at least the partial recoveries to the investors who also include the depositors even before having to wait for the final liquidation so as to achieve a smooth consumption as well as return to the investable funds to the public sooner than it would have been the case.

5.4 Conclusion

Can we be assaulted by another financial crises? The answer lies on how the government and regulators will do in response to the lessons acquired from the two major financial crises, the Great Depression of 1930, and the Great Recession of 2008. From, the two crises, various faults and mistakes that have contributed to the boom, the resulting bust cycle and the subsequent financial crisis have been identified. Inherently, to work their way out or avoid other crises in the future, there is need for the governments and regulators, then, to have more coordination in regulatory policies at a global level. Getting the government out of banking systems may also be the best way that will help the banks out of the government and letting the entrepreneurs to figure out where the resources will need to go as being guided by the market prices, profits and losses as in a free market, then there are chances that the economy will stabilize without high possibilities of it hurting itself. There is a significant need to resolve the failed institutions.

References

Agnew, Richard L. (1945). Loans to Financial Institutions by the Reconstruction Finance Corporation. Master's Thesis: University of Nebraska.

Anari, Ali, James Kolari, and Joseph R. Mason. (2005). "Bank Asset Liquidation and the Propagation of the Great Depression." Journal of Money, Credit, and Banking 37(4): 753-773.

Arellano, C., Y. Bai, P.J. Kehoe. (2010). Financial Markets and Fluctuations in Uncertainty,îStaſ report, Federal Reserve Bank of Minneapolis.

Belkin, P., Mix, D., Nelson, R.(2010). Greece's Debt Crisis: Overview, Policy Responses,and Implications. Congressional Research Service.

Bergoeing, Raphael, Patrick J. Kehoe, and Timothy J. Kehoe. (2002) "A Decade Lost and Found: Mexico and Chile in the 1980s." Review of Economic Dynamics 5: 166-205.

Bernanke, Ben S. (1983). "Nonmonetary Effects of the Financial Crisis in the Propagation of the Great Depression," American Economic Review 73 (June): 25776.

Besharove, Douglas J., & Douglas M. Call. (2010). "The Global Budget Race." Wilson Quarterly. 34(4); 38-50.

Bishop, G., Unwin, B.(2009). Appendix: European Financial Supervision: Summary of keyelements in the Commission Communication.The Federal Trust

Board of Governors of the Federal Reserve System. (1943). Banking and Monetary Statistics, 1914-1941. Washington, DC: National Capital Press.

Bragues, George. (2009). "The Ethics of U.S. Monetary Policy In Response to the Financial Crisis of 2007-2009." Libertarian Papers. 1(31); 1-26.

Burns, Helen M. (1974). The American Banking Industry and New Deal Banking Reforms, 1933-1935. Westport, Connecticut: Greenwood Press.

Calomiris, Charles W. (2008). "The Subprime Turmoil: What's Old, What's New, and What's Next." Paper prepared for presentation at the Federal Reserve Bank of Kansas City's Symposium, "Maintaining Stability in a Changing Financial System," Jackson Hole, Wyoming, August 5.

Calomiris, Charles W., and Berry Wilson. (2004). "Bank Capital and Portfolio Management: The 1930s 'Capital Crunch' and Scramble to Shed Risk," Journal of Business 77(July): 421-56.

Calomiris, Charles W., and Eugene N. White. (1994). "The Origins of Federal Deposit Insurance," in Claudia Goldin and Gary Libecap, eds., The Regulated Economy: A Historical Approach to Political Economy, Chicago: University of Chicago Press, 145-88.

Calomiris, Charles W., and Joseph R. Mason. (1997). "Contagion and Bank Failures During the Great Depression: The June 1932 Chicago Banking Panic," American Economic Review 87 (December): 863-83.

Cargill, Thomas F., and Thomas Mayer. (2006). "The Effect of changes in Reserve Requirement s during the 1930s: the Evidence from Nonmember Banks." Journal of Economic History, June.

Carmassi, J., Gros, D., Micossi, S.(2009). The Global Financial Crisis: Causes and Cures.Journal ofCommon Market Studies, 47 (5), pp. 977–996.

Centre for European Reform (CER).(2008). Beyond banking: What the financial crisis meansfor the EU?October.

Chandler, Lester V. (1971). American Monetary Policy, 1928–1941 New York: Harper & Row.

Claessens, Stijn, M. AyhanKose and Marco E. Terrones. (2008). "What Happens During Recessions, Crunches and Busts?" IMF Working Paper #08-274 (December).

Cochran, John P. (2010). "Capital In Disequilibrium: Understanding the „Great Recession' and The Potential for Recovery." Quarterly Journal of Austrian Economics. 13(3); 42-63.

Cohen, J.B.(2008). The international monetary system: diffusion and ambiguity, International Affairs. 84 (3), pp. 455-470.

Deeg, R., O'Sullivan, M.(2009). The political economy of global finance capital. WorldPolitics,

Deposit Insurance and Risk Taking in the Banking Collapse of the 1920s." Explorations in Economic History 31(July): 357-375.

Dorning, Mike. (2011). "Obama's $1.5 trillion Tax Program Exchanges Conciliation for Confrontation." Bloomberg. 20-September.

Doti, Lynne Pierson and Larry Schweikert. (1991). Banking in the American West: From the Gold Rush to Deregulation. Norman: University of Oklahoma Press.

Dubay, Curtis S. (2011). "Obama's Jobs Plan: Permanent Tax Hikes on Job Creators." The Heritage Foundation.

Dyson, K.,(ed)(2002). European States and the Euro: Europeanization, Variation, andConvergence. Oxford: Oxford University Press. Ch. 7-10.

Eastwood, R., Holmes, P., Quaglia, L.(2009). The Financial Turmoil and EU Policy Co-operation in 2008.Journal of Common Market Studies. 47 (1), pp. 63-87.

Ebersole, J.F. (1933). "One Year of the Reconstruction Finance Corporation." Quarterly Journal of Economics 47(May): 563-583.

Economic Report of the President. Transmitted to Congress, February 2011. Washington D.C.: Government Printing Office.

Eggertsson, Gauti. (2008). "Great Expectations and the End of the Depression." American Economic Review 98(4): 1476-1516.

Eichengreen, Barry, and Jeffrey Sachs. (1985). "Exchange Rates and Economic Recovery in the 1930s," Journal of Economic History 45(4): 925-946.

Eichengreen, Barry. (1992). Golden Fetters: The Gold Standard and the Great Depression, 1919-1939. New York: Oxford University Press.

Epstein, Gerald and Thomas Ferguson. (1984). "Monetary Policy, Loan Liquidation, and Industrial Conflict: The Federal Reserve and the Open Market Operations of 1932." Journal of Economic History 44(4): 957-983.

Eurointelligence. (2010). Euro area under massive speculative attack. Eurointelligence. 28 April.

European Central Bank (ECB). (2009). The financial crisis and the response of the ECB.Speech by Jean-Claude Trichet, President of the ECB at the Ceremony conferring thehonorary title of Doctor HonorisCausa at the University of National and World Economy. 12June, Sofia.

February.

Folsom Jr., Burton. (2008). New Deal or Raw Deal. New York, NY: Threshold Editions.

Foster, J.D. (2010). "Obama Tax Hikes Defended by Myths and Straw Man Arguments." The Heritage Foundation.

Friedman, Milton and Anna Schwartz. (1963). A Monetary History of the United States, 1867-1960. Princeton, NJ: Princeton University Press.

Garriga, C., R.E. Manuelli, A. Peralta-Alva. (2012): ìA Model of Price Swings in the Housing Market,îWorking Paper No. 2012-022A, Federal Reserve Bank of St. Louis.

Hague, R., Harrop, M.(2010). 8thedition. Comparative government and politics: anintroduction. Basingstoke: Palgrave Macmillan. Ch.1.

Hardy, Charles O., and Viner, Jacob. (1935). Report on the Availability of Bank Credit in the Seventh Federal Reserve District. Washington, DC: US Government Printing Office.

Harvey, D.(2006)Neo-liberalism as creative destruction.Swedish Society for Anthropologyand Geography,88B (2), pp. 145-158.

Hayek, Friedrich. (1933). Monetary Theory and the Trade Cycle. Kaldor, N., and H.M. Croome, trans. New York, NY: Sentry Press. pp.20-22.

Held, D., McGrew, A.(2007). Globalization/Anti-Globalisation: Beyond The Great Divide.Cambridge: Polity Press.Ch.5.

Henninger, Daniel. (2010). Obama's Business Buyout. Wall Street Journal Online. 25

Herkenhoß, K. F., L. E. Ohanian. (2012a): ìWhy the U.S. Economy Has Failed to Recover and What Policies Will Promote Growth.î in Government Policies and the Delayed Economic Recovery. Hoover Institution, Stanford University.

Herkenhoß, K. F., L.E. Ohanian. (2012): ìForeclosure Delay and U.S. Unemployment. Working Paper No. 2012-017, Federal Reserve Bank of St. Louis.

Hetzel, Robert L., and Ralph F. Leach. (2001). "The Treasury-Fed Accord: A New Narrative Account," Federal Reserve Bank of Richmond Economic Quarterly 87/1 (Winter).

Higgs, Robert. (2006). Depression, War, and Cold War. Oakland, Cal.: Independent Institute.

Hodson, D., Quaglia, L.(2009). European Perspectives on the Global Financial Crisis:Introduction.Journal of Common Market Studies. [online]. 47 (5), pp. 939– 953. Available at: http://onlinelibrary.wiley.com/doi/10.1111/j.1468-5965.2009.02029.x/full [Accessed 19 July 2014].

Horwitz, S. and W. Luther (2011) 'The Great Recession and its Aftermath from a Monetary Equilibrium Theory Perspective' in S. Kates (ed.) The Global Financial Crisis: What Have We Learnt? Aldershot: Edward Elgar, pp. 75-92.

Hudson, M.(2010). Europe's Fiscal Dystopia: The "New Austerity" Road to FinancialSerfdom: Massive Cutbacks in Public Spending. Centre for Research onGlobalization.

Huizinga, Harry, and Luc Laeven. (2009) "Accounting Discretion and the Reliability of Bankss Financial Accounts: Evidence from the US Mortgage Crisis." IMF Working Paper. (June).

International Monetary Fund (IMF). (2009).Global Stability Report: Market Update. 29 January. [Online] Available at:http://www.imf.org/external/pubs/ft/fmu/eng/2009/01/index.htm [Accessed 19 July 2014].

James, Cyril F. (1938). The Growth of Chicago Banks. New York: Harper & Brothers.

Johnson, Paul. (1997). A History of the American People. New York, NY: Harper Perennial.

Jones, Homer. (1940). "An Appraisal of the Rules and Procedures of Bank Supervision, 1929-39." Journal of Political Economy. April: 183-198.

Jones, Jesse H. (1951). Fifty Billion Dollars: My Thirteen Years with the RFC (19321945). The Macmillan Company: New York.

Kane, Edward (1998). "Capital Movements, Asset Values, and Banking Policy in Globalized Markets," NBER Working Paper No. 6633.

Kaufman, George G., and Steven A. Seelig. (2000). "Treatment of Depositors at Failed Banks: Implications for the Severity of Banking Crisis, Systematic Risk, and Toobig-to-fail." Working paper presented at the annual meetings of the Financial Management Association, Seattle, WA.

Keane, M., R. Rogerson. (2012). Micro and Macro Labor Supply Elasticities: A Reassessment of Conventional Wisdom, Journal of Economic Literature, American Economic Association, 50(2), 464-76.

Kehoe, T.J., K.J. Ruhl, J.B. Steinberg. (2012): A Sudden Stop to the Savings Glut and the Future of the U.S. Economy, Working paper, Federal Reserve Bank of Minneapolis.

Kehoe, Timothy, and Edward C. Prescott. (2002). "Great Depressions of the 20th Century." Review of Economic Dynamics 5: 1-18.

Kennedy, Susan Estabrook. (1973). The Banking Crisis of 1933. Lexington: University Press of Kentucky.

Keynes, John M. (1936). The General Theory of Employment, Interest, and Money. New York, NY: Hancourt, Brace & Co.

Kimmel, Lewis H. (1939). The Availability of Bank Credit, 1933-1938. National Industrial Conference Board, Inc: New York.

Klingebiel, Daniela. (1999). "The Use of Asset Management Companies in the Resolution of Banking Crises: Cross-country Experiences. Mimeo, World Bank.

Kocherlakota, N. (2012): Incomplete Labor Markets, unpublished manuscript, Federal Reserve Bank of Minneapolis.

Krueger, Anne O., and JunghoYoo. (2001). "Chaebol Capitalism and the CurrencyFinancial Crisis in Korea," NBER Conference on Currency Crises Prevention, Islamorada Florida, January.

Landvoight, T. (2011): Housing Demand During the Boom: The Role of Expectations and Credit Constraints, unpublished manuscript, Stanford University

Leamer, E.E. (2007). Housing is the Business Cycle, Proceedings, Federal Reserve Bank of Kansas City, 149-233.

Lee, Dwight R. (1986). Taxation and the Deficit Economy. San Francisco, Cal.: Pacific Research Institute.

Liu Z, Wang P, T. Zha. (2011): Land-Price Dynamics and Macroeconomic Fluctuations, Working paper, Federal Reserve Bank of San Francisco.

Manuelli, R.E., A. Peralta-Alva. (2011): Sectoral Shocks, Reallocation Frictions, and Optimal Government Spending, Working Paper No. 2011-017, Federal Reserve Bank of Saint Louis.

Mason, Joseph R. (2001a). "Do Lender of Last Resort Policies Matter? The Effects of

Mason, Joseph R. (2001b). "Reconstruction Finance Corporation Assistance to Financial Institutions and Commercial & Industrial Enterprise in the

US Great Depression, 1932 – 1937." In Resolution of Financial Distress, StijnClaessens, Simeon Djankov, and AshokaMody, eds. Washington: World Bank Press, pp. 167-204.

Mason, Joseph R. (2005). "A Real Options Approach to Bankruptcy Costs: Evidence from Failed Commercial Banks during the 1990s." Journal of Business 79(3): 152353.

Mason, Joseph R. (2009). "The Evolution of the Reconstruction Finance Corporation as a Lender of Last Resort in the Great Depression," in Bailouts and Government Rescues, Robert E. Wright, ed. New York: SSRC/Columbia University Press.

Mayes, D.G.(2009). Did Recent Experience of a Financial Crisis Help inCoping with theCurrent Financial Turmoil? The Case of the Nordic Countries.Journal of Common MarketStudies. 47 (5). pp. 997–1015.

McCormick, J.(2007). The European Superpower.Basingstoke: Palgrave Macmillan. Ch. 5.

McDonald, J.F. (1981): Capital-Land Substitution in Urban Housing: A Survey of Empirical Estimates, Journal of Urban Economics, 9(2), 190-11.

McGowen, James C. (1977). The Reconstruction Finance Corporation: some historical perspective. Center for the Study of American Business, Washington University 3(11).

Meltzer, Allan. (2003). A History of the Federal Reserve. Chicago, IL: University of Chicago Press.

Miller, John. (1931). "The National Credit Corporation." Investment Banking. 2(December 2): 53-7.

Mises, Ludwig von. (1983). Bureaucracy. Spring Mills, Pen: Libertarian Press, Inc.

Nanto, K.D.(2009). The Global Financial Crisis: Analysis and Policy Implications.[Online] Congressional Research Service. Available at:http://assets.opencrs.com/rpts/RL34742_20090403.pdf[Accessed 16 July 2014].

Ohanian, L. E., A. Raso. (2012): iAggregate Hours Worked in OECD Countries: New Measurement and Implications for Business Cycles, Journal of Monetary Economics, Carnegie NYU-Rochester Conference Series on Public Policy, 59(1), 40-56.

Olson, James S. (1972a). From Depression to Defense: The Reconstruction Finance Corporation: 1932-1940. Dissertation: State University of New York at Stony Brook, 1972a.

Olson, James S. (1977). Herbert Hoover and the Reconstruction Finance Corporation, 1931-1933. Ames, Iowa: Iowa State University Press.

Olson, James S. (1988). Saving Capitalism. Princeton: Princeton University Press.

Olson, James Stuart. (1972b). "The End of Voluntarism: Herbert Hoover and the National Credit Corporation." Annals of Iowa. 41(Fall): 1104-1113.

Panzer, Michael J. (2008). Financial Armageddon. New York, NY: Kaplan Publishing.

Reconstruction Finance Corporation Assistance to Banks During the Great Depression," Journal of Financial Services Research 20 (September): 77-95.

Reconstruction Finance Corporation. (1932). RFC Circular no. 4. Washington, DC: US Government Printing Office.

Reinhart, Carmen M. and Kenneth Rogoff. (2009). "The Aftermath of Financial Crises," American Economic Review 99 (May): 466-472

Rockoff, Hugh. (1993). "The Meaning of Money in the Great Depression." NBER Historical Paper #52.

Romer, "What Ended the Great Depression?" Journal of Economic History 52(4): 757784.

Romer, Christina. (1990). "The Great Crash and the Onset of the Great Depression." Quarterly Journal of Economics. August: 597-624.

Romer, Christina. (2009). "Lessons from the Great Depression for Economic Recovery in 2009." Policy Speech at the Brookings Institution, March 9. http://www.brookings.edu/~/media/Files/events/2009/0309_lessons/0309_lessons_ro mer.pdf

Rothbard, M. N. (1963). America's great depression. Princeton NJ: D. Van Nostrand Company, Inc.

Rothbard, Murray N. (1963). America's Great Depression. Princeton NJ: D. Van Nostrand Company, Inc.

Schwartz, Anna J. (1992). "The Misuse of the Fed's Discount Window." Federal Reserve Bank of St. Louis Review, September/October 74(5): 58-69.

Simonson, Donald G., and George H. Hemple. "Banking Lessons From the Past: The 1938 Regulatory Agreement Interpreted." Journal of Financial Services Research. 1993, pp. 249-267.

Stiglitz, Joseph, and Andrew Weiss. (1981). "Credit Rationing in Markets with Imperfect Information. American Economic Review 71(3): 393-410.

Sullivan, Francis J. (1951). Reconstruction Finance Corporation and Corporate Financial Policy. Thesis: George Washington University.

Temin, Peter and Barrie Wigmore. (1990). "The End of One Big Deflation." Explorations in Economic History 27(October): 483-502.

Temin, Peter. (1989). Lessons from the Great Depression. Cambridge MA: MIT Press.

Thornton, M. (2010). Hoover, Bush and Great depressions. *Quarterly Journal of Austrian Economics,* 13(3): 86-100.

Upham, Cyril B., and Edwin Lamke. (1934). Closed and Distressed Banks: A Study in Public Administration. Washington, DC: The Brookings Institution.

Walk, Everett G. (1937). "Loans of Federal Agencies and their Relationship to the Capital Market." Dissertation, University of Pennsylvania.

Wheelock, D.C. (1992). Monetary policy in the great depression: What the Fed did, and why. *Federal Reserve Bank of St. Louis Review.* 74 (2).

Wheelock, David C., and Subal C. Kumbhakar. (1994). "'The Slack Banker Dances':

Wicker, Elmus. (1966). Federal Reserve Monetary Policy 1917–1933. New York: Random House.

Wigmore, Barrie A. (1985). The Crash and its Aftermath; A History of Security Markets in the United States, 1929-1933. Westport, CT: Greenwood Press.

www.ingramcontent.com/pod-product-compliance
Lightning Source LLC
Chambersburg PA
CBHW030840180526
45163CB00004B/1390